THE VOICE
POVERTY
CANNOT
SILENCE

DESTITUTE
ISN'T DESTINY

MIQUETTE
MCMAHON

CONTENTS

For my Mother, Rose
For John and Mary Lee
In memory of my Papa, Bos Clé

—

And for every poor child around the world—
don't let poverty silence your dreams

FOREWORD

IN THE FIRST month of my first year as president of Concordia College, a young graduate knocked on my office door. I have never forgotten our conversation. Miquette Denie McMahon, who had come to Minnesota on a fundraising visit, told me of her journey from abject poverty in Haiti, to an unexpected chance for high school study in the United States, to commencement from Concordia in 2006 and return to her native country with a bachelor's degree in nursing. And there, compelled by her own experience and the all but impossible odds for Haitian children growing up as she had done, she founded a school.

In a harsh world, where the poor stay poor, often for generations, hers was the kind of story we long to hear: a story of parental sacrifice, childhood wonder and struggle, determination in the face of prejudice and loss, and above all, faith in the grace of God. That summer in 2011, only in my new job long enough to feel its mystery and promise, I was all but overwhelmed by the radiance of Miquette's narrative. I somehow managed a question: What difference had Concordia made in her life? All but certain that I knew what her answer would be—that Concordia had enabled her to be the first person in the history of her family to attend college and to graduate—I got my second joyful surprise of the day. She did not give the answer I expected. Instead, she told me, "Concordia taught me to dream bigger dreams." Dreams, she meant, for the lives of others.

You will soon read her story, one that takes you to a country of great beauty and great suffering, a place where families work to eat so that they can survive to work and eat again, a place where so many do not make it out of childhood, and where so many who do find pathways to security and opportunity blocked by class bias and a lack of education to navigate and overcome it. And yet, from her grandmother to her parents to a Minnesota pastor's family who saw her great gifts and joined with her Haitian family to give Miquette a chance at a transformed life, this is above all a story of love that affirms the dignity of every child of God.

Once you start reading, keep your calendar clear: you will not be able to set this book aside. Miquette's is a story of a "voice that poverty cannot silence." That in itself would be enough, but by the time you finish her book, you will see that because of Miquette, there are other voices now no longer silent: the voices of teachers and staff at Teach Haiti, the school that she founded; the voices of those in the United States who support them; and most wonderful, the voices of the Haitian children set free to claim the promise of their lives and become the hope of a nation.

Retired now from Concordia, I can say that I have met again and again remarkable graduates doing work both good and great. They embody the mission of the college to "influence the affairs of the world by sending into society thoughtful and informed men and women dedicated to the Christian life." Miquette is an extraordinary one of them, one who shines out in living by faith in the still small voice of God, who calls us to dream bigger dreams by loving our neighbors as ourselves.

William Craft, President Emeritus, Concordia College

"For I know the plans I have for you," says the LORD.

JEREMIAH 29:11 (NLT)

INTRODUCTION

IT IS BY the grace of God that I am able to write this book.

I am from a small town called St. Michel de L'Attalaye located on the Caribbean island of Haiti. I was born a poor girl, but I always had big dreams. This is my story and the story of those who molded me into the person I am today. My goal is to highlight their strength and struggles as they persevered in giving me a better life—an opportunity that ultimately changed the future of my entire family.

This book is dedicated to every child around the world who is on a quest for a better life. It is for the poor child who lies awake at night, wondering if it's time to give up on their dreams. It is for the child who, despite the beatdowns life has dealt them, refuses to stop believing.

This book is for the child who dares to hope, who clings to the belief that as long as there is breath in their lungs, there is still a chance—still a possibility—that their dreams can come true.

Every child who has ever felt unseen, unheard, or unworthy—this is for you. May you find in these pages a reflection of your own strength and a spark of inspiration to keep chasing your dreams, no matter how impossible they may seem.

No matter where you start, your dreams are valid, and your story matters.

Throughout these pages is a journey through pain and triumph, a testament to the power of faith, determination, and the kindness of people who choose to invest in others. You'll learn about the incredible people who shaped my life—their unwavering spirit and their relentless pursuit of a brighter future. I invite you to walk with me on this journey, to experience the ups and downs and to discover the triumphs that come from perseverance and love.

In sharing my story, I also hope to illuminate the beauty and resilience of Haiti, my homeland. Though often misunderstood, it is a place filled with vibrant culture, indomitable people, and stories of hope. Through the lens of my personal experiences, I wish to paint a picture of the Haiti that I know and love—a place where dreams are born, and possibilities are endless.

As you turn the pages, may you find solace in knowing that no matter how dark the night, the dawn will always come. Let this book be a beacon of light, a reminder that every challenge is an opportunity to rise stronger and more determined than before.

Thank you, dear reader, for opening this book and allowing me to share my story, my beautiful family, and my country with you. I hope you will find hope in these pages. My desire is that this book will inspire you, especially if you are going through a difficult time.

Together, let's explore the power of faith, family, and the enduring human spirit.

PART ONE

Just a Poor Girl

CHAPTER 1

"Wow, Gadon Coquette!"

"MIQUETTE, WHEN IS your birthday?" Mommy Carme asked me one day.

Her voice was soft but probing, as though she was uncovering a small mystery about me that no one else had bothered to explore. I froze, embarrassed and unsure of how to respond.

"I don't know," I admitted, my voice barely above a whisper. The truth was, no one had ever asked me before.

Mommy Carme smiled, her eyes brimming with warmth. "Oh, Miquette," she said, "it's an important part of who you are. Go find out your birthday, and once you do, a gift will be here waiting for you." Her words gently nudged me toward a journey into my past—one that would lead me to a truth I had never fully known.

At the age of sixteen, I discovered I was born on June 8, 1980, around 10 p.m.—or so we think. In our home, there was no clock, no watch to mark the passing of time. My birth was etched into memory not by its precise timing but by the quiet of the evening, illuminated by the flickering glow of a *tèt gridap*—a lamp fashioned from an empty milk can with a kerosene-soaked wick.

My mama told me my father's face lit up with pride. "Wow, *gadon coquette*!" he exclaimed, calling me a "charming child." His words, filled with love and delight, inspired my mama to name me Miquette.

I was born into a humble house of mud and sticks, held together by hope and resilience. Two small rooms made up our entire world. My parents shared one, its twin bed and small bedside table holding their most precious belongings. In the corner, a *kanari*—or clay jar—stood as our water storage, keeping its contents cool in the oppressive heat.

The second room was where my siblings and I slept. There were no beds, just a woven mat of banana leaves called a *nat* and a pile of tattered clothes that served as makeshift bedding. We lay so close to one another at night that it felt as though we were stitched together, every breath and movement a reminder of the bond we shared.

But nights were not always easy. Once darkness fell, the door was shut, and venturing outside was forbidden. The night belonged to the *lougarou*, the bogeyman of village folklore, said to prey on children foolish enough to wander. Even the thought of stepping outside to our backyard's latrine—a hole in the ground surrounded by rags for privacy—sent chills down my spine. I had heard stories of children falling into latrines, their cries echoing in the night. Those fears were enough to keep me firmly rooted on the nat.

Inside, our only light came from the small lamp tèt gridap. But even this flickering flame was a luxury. On many nights, we couldn't afford kerosene or wicks, and the house was plunged into darkness. My brother Pidens, ever the mischief-maker, took advantage of these moments. Pretending to be the lougarou, he made eerie noises that sent me cowering deeper into the nat, tears streaming down my face as he laughed.

This was my world—a world without electricity, running water, or indoor plumbing. Growing up, it was all I had ever known, so I didn't question it. It was our normal, even if it meant enduring hardships others couldn't imagine. Life in our little house was tough and simple, yet it was rich with laughter, courage, and hope. Within those humble walls, joy still found a way to fill our hearts.

Joy lived in the ordinary—in mangoes, avocados, oranges, and kenepes that fell freely from the trees in our yard, each one a small gift from nature. Just beyond the yard, a sugar cane field stretched behind our house, where we played hide and seek until the sun dipped below the hills. Our dolls were made of rags and imagination, yet to us, they were beautiful and full of life.

Joy was woven into the rhythm of family, in the comfort of a good Sunday meal: steaming rice topped with bean sauce and on our luckiest days, a small portion of meat. We didn't have much, and some days we had nothing at all, but we still had enough to smile. Enough to dream.

Despite their poverty, my parents made sure we felt cherished. My mama saved for the best-embroidered towels and tiny dresses, and my father did all he could to ensure she had nourishing food during her pregnancies. These small gestures, born from great sacrifice, spoke volumes of their love. My parents dreamed that one day, one of their children might rise above the hardships they endured and create a new life.

Looking back, I see the extraordinary in what seemed ordinary. I see the strength of my parents' sacrifices, the courage in their daily struggles, and the beauty in the laughter that filled our modest home. My story didn't begin in grandeur but in the amazing love of family.

It was in that house of mud and sticks, under the faint glow of a tèt gridap lamp, that my journey began. When I finally discovered the date of my birth, I returned to tell Mommy Carme. True to her word, she gave me a beautiful sundress—a gift that symbolized so much more than a birthday. It was a celebration of identity, of belonging, and of reclaiming a part of myself I never knew I was missing.

But there's so much more to the story. And to truly understand the adversity I overcame and the sacrifices we all made, it's important to introduce some of the key heroes in my journey. I'd like to start with my mama, the strongest woman I know.

MEET MY MAMA

My mama Rose was born on July 15, 1950, into a family with several children, but she was the only one who survived past the age of ten. She was the third child, but her older brother Stevio died at the age of ten from an unknown ailment, and her second brother also passed away at a young age. So did three other siblings after her. Because of this, my mama became the pride and joy of her parents, who adored her immensely. Her father's name was Estagne with a nickname "Tinyo," and her mama's was Saint Julia, but everyone called her "Bouboute." Her parents saw my mama's survival as a blessing, a light in their lives that had been marred by tragedy and loss.

My mama's family was extremely poor. Her father was a farmer, and all of their food came directly from the land. They lived in a small hut in the middle of a three-acre sugar cane field. The hut was modest, with walls made from mud and sticks and a thatched roof that barely kept the rain out during the wet season. This was their home, a place of both hard work and uncertainty about the future. Yet, for my mama, it was a sanctuary filled with dreams of a better life she yearned for herself and her future children.

By the age of five, my mama was already contributing to the family's sustenance. Every morning, she would go to the field to gather sugar cane. The process was laborious; she would carefully cut the cane and carry it back to their hut. Afterward, she would dig up sweet potatoes from the ground, dirt clinging to her hands as she worked. She would then bring them home to boil with sour oranges. This simple meal was often accompanied by avocado, the creamy flesh providing a rich contrast to the rustic flavors of the farm's bounty.

In the afternoons, she would gather corn and spinach from her front yard. It was a routine born out of necessity. She was very resourceful. Dinner was usually *tchaka*, a traditional Haitian dish made with beans, corn, pumpkin, and sometimes scraps of meat if they were lucky. Many times, there was no meat at all, but the hearty combination of vegetables made for a satisfying meal. The smell of tchaka simmering over an open fire was a comfort on many long, hard days.

Despite her hunger for knowledge, my mama was never sent to school. Her father, lacking money and believing a girl's role was to find a husband, saw no value in her education. It was a common belief, but it left her longing for more. She often watched the village children walking to school—some of them girls, though far fewer than boys—and wondered what it would be like to learn, grow, and one day break free from poverty.

By six, my mama's daily chores included selling sugar cane door to door. Balancing ten canes on her head, she walked to the *bourg*, the town square where most people with money lived, earning 50 *kob* (a nickel) per trip. Each sale meant an hour-long barefoot walk back to the plantation under the scorching sun, navigating spiky rocks, broken glass, and debris. She did this three times a day, earning 15 cents, with no time to rest. It was exhausting, but it was all she knew.

For a while, she held onto a small hope that her father might change his mind and send her to school. But by the time she turned ten, that hope began to fade. She realized it wasn't going to happen. While her peers proudly wore uniforms, shared stories about their school day, and learned to read and write, she stayed home, tending to chores and selling sugar cane three times a day.

Her home was often filled with tension, shaped by her parents' opposing beliefs. Her mother, Bouboute, was a devoted Christian, while her father, Tinyo, relied on voodoo for protection. When my mama fell gravely ill at ten, Grandpa took her to a *bòkor* (a voodoo priest), believing she was cursed. She was meant to stay in the *badji* (temple) until healed, but Grandma, upon discovering this, walked two hours to take her home, trusting in God's power instead. Furious, Grandpa blamed her for risking their daughter's life, escalating their conflict.

My mama never knew where Grandma's faith came from—she certainly did not have any role model of faith in her home—but she is grateful to have had a godly woman as her mother. Though illiterate, her mother taught her about God using His creation— the oceans, the trees, and all the wonders of the world He made. She encouraged my mama to go to church on Sundays, even when her father protested, but she never gave up. My mama hung on every word, and that devotion stirred something deep within her at a young age. She longed to have what her mother had, and she resolved that, no matter what, she too would follow God.

As a result, the household became a battleground of faith and fear. Grandpa's threats turned to violence, forcing Grandma to leave. She struggled to earn enough to reclaim her children. In the end, poverty forced her to return them to Grandpa's care, but she made the painful decision not to stay herself. That choice, though heartbreaking, became a defining moment—one that deepened my mama's resilience and fortified her faith.

After recovering from her illness, her faith in Jesus took root, and from that day on, she chose her path with conviction to follow Him wholeheartedly.

My mama's spirit remained unbroken, and she began to dream of a better future.

She resolved early on to ensure her children would attend school, something she had never experienced. She dreamed of them becoming doctors, nurses, teachers, and leaders who would make a difference in the world. She told me she wanted more than survival; she longed for a world where education was a right, not a privilege, and her children could access the opportunities she never had. Her vision wasn't just about a better life for herself or her family; it was about creating a legacy of empowerment and change.

Even as a young girl, my mama knew the path would be arduous, but her resolve was as steadfast as the Haitian sun. That dream became her driving force, fueling her daily life and giving her the strength to persevere against insurmountable odds.

Often left at home to fend for herself, my mama, at only ten and a half years old, knew she had to act to help her family, so she sought work. Through prayer and persistence, she found an opportunity.

She decided to reach out to a woman named Leonne, who was a cook for a well-known deputy in the bourg. She went to the deputy's house and waited anxiously in the corridor, anticipating Leonne's return from the *maché* (market) with her groceries. When Leonne passed by, Mom stopped her and boldly introduced herself:

"My name is Rose. I am the daughter of Tinyo and Saint Julia." She did her best to make a good impression by showing her confidence.

Leonne, known as the best cook in the village and admired for working for prominent families like the deputy's, was intrigued. In a place where most girls avoided eye contact, here was a young girl unafraid to step into a world of prestige.

Mom continued, "I may be young, but I'm a hard worker. I want to learn to cook, and I know you can teach me. Please help me."

She believed that every woman should know how to cook—not only to care for her future family but also to have a skill that could bring income and independence. She was determined to learn from the best.

At first, Leonne hesitated, unsure what to make of this bold and determined child. But she took a chance—and that decision changed everything.

A DIFFERENT WORLD

Leonne made it clear from the start: nothing would be handed to my mama. "You have to earn your spot here," she said firmly. "I don't work with lazy people. I serve important people every day. Don't embarrass me."

Mom promised Leonne she was a hard worker and would follow every instruction. Leonne, impressed by her persistence and boldness, allowed Mom to start by scrubbing and washing the cooking pots, offering her 5 gourdes a month—about $1, a sharp decline from the better wages she once brought home selling sugar cane. But for Mama, this wasn't just a job but a chance to prove she could rise above her circumstances.

Determined to excel, Mom learned how to scrub the pots with *paille de fer* (steel wool), cleaning every corner until they gleamed. She thought she was making great progress, but Leonne was not impressed.

"This isn't good enough," she said, dissatisfied with the results. Eventually, Leonne told her she couldn't keep her and had already hired someone else for the job.

Desperate to stay, Mom pleaded with her. "Don't fire me. Let me stay and continue learning from you. You don't have to pay me—I'll do it for free."

Leonne, once more, moved by her determination, reluctantly agreed. Although unpaid, Mom kept scrubbing pots while quietly observing how Leonne cooked and prepared meals for the deputy. She also watched Joseph, the butler, as he meticulously set the table each day, taking mental notes on every detail—from the placement of forks and knives to the precise arrangement of dishes.

One day, Joseph fell ill and couldn't come to work. Leonne, overwhelmed with other tasks, didn't have time to set the table and grew visibly stressed. Seeing this, Mom stepped forward. "I can set the table," she offered.

Leonne was skeptical. "You? Are you sure?"

Mom nodded confidently. "I've watched Joseph every day. I know how it's done."

Reluctantly, but with no better option, Leonne agreed—and Mom's chance to prove herself had finally arrived. Mom set the table perfectly, replicating every detail she had observed from Joseph. Each piece of cutlery was in its proper place, the plates and glasses arranged precisely, and the napkins folded in Joseph's intricate style. When Leonne saw the table, she was astonished. Everything was flawless. Pleased and impressed, Leonne thanked her profusely and immediately reinstated her on the payroll—this time with a higher wage.

This success was a turning point for Mom. No longer just helping out, she became an integral part of the household staff. Her newfound responsibility gave her a sense of pride and accomplishment.

Mom was captivated by the deputy's house—it was unlike anything she had ever seen. The grand two-story home, adorned with fine furniture, art, and an air of sophistication, felt worlds away from the modest hut she called home. The elegant dining room, the intricately decorated living spaces, and even the smallest details transported her into a different reality.

Leonne's cooking was exceptional, unlike anything Mom had ever tasted. The table overflowed with neatly arranged dishes—grains, meats, vegetables, and fresh fruits—offering guests the freedom to take as much or as little as they liked. It was a stark contrast to her home, where meals were simple, often meager, and shared from small plastic bowls. Meat was a rare luxury, and every meal was more about survival than indulgence.

Yet, the true allure of the deputy's house was not just the lavish surroundings or abundant food—it was the conversations. The home was a hub of influence, a meeting place for politicians, intellectuals, and community leaders whose discussions opened a window into a world far beyond her own.

Mom was fascinated by how the family dined—sitting around the table, effortlessly using forks, knives, and spoons—and by the topics they discussed. Although she wasn't allowed in the room during these conversations, she found hidden spots where she could quietly listen. She admired how they laughed, shared stories, and enjoyed one another's company. She was mesmerized by their vocabulary, filled with words she had never heard, and their stories of travels to distant places like the United States, Canada, and Europe. They debated politics, shared economic strategies, and exchanged ideas that could shape the future of Haiti.

Despite the inspiration she found in their world, Mom had to grow a thick skin to survive. The household imposed strict rules on the workers they considered beneath them. Everyone had to be impeccably clean, wash their hands repeatedly, and wear a bonnet in the dining room. She couldn't afford to be seen as vulnerable, yet she often felt humiliated by the deputy's children. Some were her age, others older, but all treated her with disdain, as though her poverty made her invisible—or worse, unwelcome. The children never spoke to Mom except to bark orders, making it clear she was there only to serve them.

Their selfishness stung the most. Instead of being offered to the workers, leftovers were deliberately spoiled. The children would smear sticky mango peels across the food, letting the fibrous residue and juice seep in. The sweet scent turned sour when mixed with savory dishes, leaving the food soggy, stained, and unappetizing. The children knew the workers would treasure those leftovers, but they ruined them out of spite. Still, the workers, including Mom, refused to be defeated. They would pick off the mango peels, salvage what they could, and bring the food home.

Mom's family eagerly awaited her return at six o'clock every evening, knowing she would bring home treasures from the *gwo zotobre's* (rich folks) house —dishes like rice and beans, salad, vegetables, and most luxuriously, meat. These meals starkly contrasted their usual fare of cornmeal and vegetables. Every bite was savored, offering a rare moment of indulgence and comfort in their otherwise simple lives. She often wished she could save some meat for the next day or Sunday when most families enjoyed their best meals. But without electricity or a fridge, preserving food was impossible. The lack of modern conveniences was a daily battle against hunger and poverty.

My mama saw the stark disparity between her world and theirs, but the humiliation and hard work didn't break her spirit. In the kitchen, she absorbed everything she could from Leonne, observing her cooking techniques and learning skills she hoped would one day serve her well. Each evening, she returned home with tales of the big house—stories of the meals she prepared, the elegance of the dining table, and the lives of the people she served. Her three younger siblings listened in awe, captivated by the world she described, so far removed from their own.

The time spent at the deputy's house ignited a hunger in my mama for something greater. It became a refuge that broadened her perspective and fueled her dreams. She longed for an education that could unlock a world like theirs. She envisioned a future where her children could go to school and where meals were more than sustenance but moments to gather, celebrate, and thrive. It gave her ambition and strengthened her resolve to create a better future for herself and her family.

Even at ten and a half, she believed that being destitute didn't define her destiny.

Throughout her life, my mother embodied the hope and strength many in our village clung to. She taught me that with perseverance and faith, even the most daunting challenges could be faced head-on. And as you continue to learn about her, you will see how her ambition for a brighter future for herself and her children came at a tremendous cost—sacrifices so profound that few could genuinely fathom their depth.

Her story reminds me that even in the face of adversity, the human spirit is capable of incredible strength and resilience. Her story reminds me that no dream is too big and no circumstance too small to transform a life. And no matter how tough life gets, there is always a chance for a brighter tomorrow—a belief she passed on to me. Because she dared to dream beyond our circumstances, I learned to dream big, too.

CHAPTER 2

Meet My Papa

MY PAPA'S STORY begins in a remote village in Marmelade, a community located in the department of Artibonite. Life for him and his siblings was incredibly harsh and primitive. Similar to my mama, his family lived in a small hut made of mud sticks and a thatched roof, and they survived on what they could grow on their farm. He and his siblings slept on the floor while their parents shared the only twin bed in the house. They had no tables or chairs, and they used a kanari to store drinking water. It provided a brief respite from the heat, offering cool water that refreshed them after long hours of labor in the fields.

Though life was harsh and unforgiving, the landscape of my papa's surroundings were picturesque, with lush greenery contrasting with the challenging conditions of daily life. The sun beat down relentlessly during the dry season, while the rainy season turned the paths to mud, making even simple tasks a struggle.

Similar to my mom, my papa's family came from generational poverty; no one in his family had ever attended school. All his siblings, cousins, and extended family members were farmers who harvested and sold their produce in the village. They would rise before the sun and work the fields with their bare hands—planting and harvesting whatever crops they could manage. They were at the mercy of the land and the weather, hoping each season would yield enough to sustain them. Though life was tough for my papa and his siblings, he still enjoyed his childhood. He loved playing soccer with makeshift balls, usually crafted from old rags.

Papa's village was very isolated from the rest of the country and hard to reach. It was several hours' walk to the bourg of Marmelade, where life was a bit more civilized. According to his parents, the trip to the bourg was dangerous because of the treacherous roads, with more than 100-foot drops on both sides. The narrow roads were lined with jagged rocks that resembled spikes. His parents dreaded the journey, but for Papa and his siblings, traveling to the bourg was an exciting adventure. He loved seeing the homes with tin roofs and people buying rice, beans, and other luxurious foods like meat. And he loved seeing children riding their bikes.

Papa was also especially fascinated by the cars, which he only saw when visiting the bourg. In his village, people used donkeys for transportation and to carry goods to the maché. Papa's family couldn't afford to own donkeys, but those who had some money could. Fortunately, his village was a community that shared resources. In dire circumstances, Papa's parents would borrow a neighbor's donkey for special trips, especially if it involved taking a sick child to see a nurse.

Papa often dreamed of a life outside his village, and he frequently wondered how kids outside his village lived. *Did they have huts like his family? Did they all farm? Did they eat mostly vegetables, like his family did?*

One day, when Papa was about ten years old, he was outside in the scorching sun after a long day of work on the farm when he encountered a man from St. Michel. Impressed by my papa's physique and stamina, the man asked about his parents. Upon learning who they were, the man expressed a desire to meet them, and my papa promptly led him to his family.

The man introduced himself, claiming to have an impressive résumé. He was probably the most affluent man who had ever visited my papa's parents, and they were impressed. His presence was commanding, and his clothes were finer than anything my papa had seen. He was a judge, and he requested that Papa come with him to live in St. Michel, promising Papa would be well-fed, clothed, and educated. Though he never clearly stated what Papa's duties would be, it went without saying that he would be responsible for many household chores.

Papa was filled with glee. St. Michel was several hours away from Marmelade, but Papa couldn't wait to leave his village. His family had very little, so he started dreaming of all the nice things he would see there and all the food he would eat regularly. He imagined plates filled with rice, beans, and especially meat. He dreamed of all the exotic dishes he had only heard stories about. Most importantly, Papa thought about how fun it would be to finally go to school—to be the first in his family to experience an education. Papa dreamed of how different things would be from what he had known for the first ten years of his life. He thought about how much he would miss his family, but his excitement was more powerful than the fear of being away from them.

His parents agreed to let Papa go with the judge, and in 1943, my papa embarked on the journey to St. Michel. Tears streamed down his parents' and siblings' faces as they embraced him one last time, wondering when—or if—they would see him again. The journey home, if it ever came, would take hours, but for now, he was stepping into the unknown.

When he arrived at the judge's house, he was struck with awe. The grand structure, with its multiple rooms and gleaming tin roof, was a world away from the humble hut he had always called home. It stood like a monument to possibility, a symbol of everything he had dreamed of but never dared to believe could be his.

Papa gazed at the house with wonder, his heart swelling with hope. He was on the brink of a new life—a life that held more than a diet of vegetables and farming for scraps. Here, under the guardianship of a judge, was a future filled with learning, growth, and the promise of success. For the first time, Papa felt like the road ahead was leading him somewhere extraordinary.

Papa liked the neighborhood, too. It was one of the more affluent areas in St. Michel called Rue Guerrier, which was known for its residents who owned businesses and had better schools for their children, and the homes even had maids and yardmen to care for the families and properties. Papa was in awe of this new environment, so different from his village, and he couldn't wait to start enjoying all the promises the judge had made to his parents—especially attending *school*.

But when Papa arrived, those promises unraveled into nothing but a devastating, heart-wrenching, *big fat lie*.

Instead of stepping into a life of opportunity, he was plunged into a nightmare of backbreaking labor and unrelenting despair. Instead of an escape, he found himself trapped in a cage of exploitation, deceit, and broken promises. Each day, he toiled like a slave, hauling heavy buckets of water to fill 55-gallon drums, his dreams evaporating with every step. The promise of education and a better life was shattered, replaced with grueling tasks and days filled with the monotonous routine of servitude.

The judge's grand, elegant house stood as a mocking reminder of what could never be his. Despite its many spacious rooms, Papa was cast aside, deemed unworthy to sleep under its roof. He was relegated to a dusty corner outside the kitchen, filled with soot from the charcoal stove. His bed was nothing more than a tattered mat made from banana leaves on the cold, hard floor. On colder nights, when the air bit through his thin clothes, there were no blankets, no warmth—just the bitter realization that he was utterly alone.

The truth settled over him like a suffocating weight. The life he had dared to dream of was nothing more than a cruel illusion, and his spirit fought to survive the crushing betrayal. Oh, how he longed to go back to his family and his modest life in Marmelade!

Although the promise of sending my papa to school was a lie, he was grateful when, at sixteen, he was granted a small measure of freedom to become an apprentice. On Saturdays, he learned carpentry skills from a local craftsman, Boss Meius. Yet, this privilege came at a cost—he still had to complete all his daily chores, the same grueling workload as any other day. His story reminds me of the Israelites under Pharaoh's rule, toiling endlessly with no relief.

But my papa understood the value of learning a trade. Without one, he knew most parents wouldn't allow him to marry their daughters. So he pushed himself to finish his work, determined not to give the judge any reason to revoke his rare opportunity to learn. He was keenly aware that his worth in that household was measured solely by the labor he provided. Though they treated him like a slave, he found ways to be grateful.

My papa said that working with Boss Meius was the best thing that came out of living with the judge. Papa focused on polishing his skills as a carpenter, and despite being illiterate, he became a great student and learned a great deal. Although he had to work extra hard to balance his chores and apprenticeship, he felt a sense of pride and purpose, and even when exhaustion threatened to break him, he worked tirelessly, knowing that this skill could one day be his escape.

BOY MEETS GIRL

One sweltering summer afternoon, as my mom made her way home from her job at the deputy's house, she unknowingly caught the eye of a determined young man—my papa. She was beautiful—she walked with grace and quiet confidence and carried herself with dignity. There was a strength in her spirit and a spark in her eyes that intrigued him. She wasn't trying to be noticed, but that's exactly what made her unforgettable.

But my mama had her eye on another boy and wanted nothing to do with Papa. She even refused to reveal where she lived, knowing her parents would likely favor Papa over the boy she secretly admired. Despite her efforts to keep him at a distance, Papa's persistence paid off. He discovered her home and boldly took the next step.

Dating in our village required a few extra steps than most are accustomed to today: To show respect, a man had to first seek the approval of the girl's parents, preferably the dad, before even speaking to her. Eager to win my mama over, Papa met with her father.

With a strong clear voice, he declared his intentions: "I am a carpenter. I can take care of your daughter." It was a straight-forward yet profound promise, reflective of the values of their time—responsibility, respect, and the earnest pursuit of love. In those days, having a trade meant stability, which was exactly what parents looked for. And as my mama feared, her parents were indeed impressed by Papa's determination and potential.

At sixteen, my mom began her courtship with my papa. She didn't fall in love with Papa right away. In fact, romance was the furthest thing from her mind. But over time, she began to admire him—not for grand gestures but for his quiet strength, work ethic, and the steady way he showed up each day. He wasn't flashy or smooth with words, but he was dependable, hardwork-ing, and kind.

As they spent more time in each other's presence—whether at church, in the market, or during village gatherings—she began to see something deeper in him: a vision for the future. She realized that with him, she could build a life of security and partner-ship—something she had never known.

With the blessings of their families, they planned to marry when she turned twenty. However, by the age of eighteen, she was preg-nant with their first child. She dreamed of a wedding, but her father couldn't afford one, so the dream had to wait.

Wilfrid, their firstborn, changed everything. From the moment they knew he was coming, they poured every ounce of love, hope, and determination into preparing for his arrival. There were no ultrasounds, no doctor visits—all mama and papa had was faith and fierce devotion.

When my mama began showing, she lost her job at the deputy's house. In the eyes of her employer, a pregnant teenage girl was seen as a liability—especially in a position of domestic work. Her world felt smaller that day. She had counted on that job to help build a better future for her baby. But she didn't give up. She juggled three jobs at once, waking before dawn and coming home after sunset. Her hands were raw from washing clothes, and her feet ached from the long hours, and yet, she kept going. Every shift, every coin she earned, was for Wilfrid. But none of it was steady, and none of it was ever enough.

Papa struggled, too. Work was sparse and unpredictable. Carpentry jobs came and went like rain showers—here one moment, gone the next. Still, he kept showing up and searching for work, not just for himself but for the family he'd vowed to care for. His promise to my grandfather sat heavy on his heart, and each missed opportunity felt like he was breaking that vow.

Wilfrid was born in 1968 on a dirt floor, delivered by Yet, a local *femme sage*. He was a lively, joyful baby, cherished beyond measure by my parents. They carried him everywhere, their unshakable bond shining for all to see. Wilfrid was their treasure and pride. My parents clung to each other and to Wilfrid, the little boy who made them believe that, even in a world of struggle, love could still feel like heaven.

Their love was fierce, their dreams big—but love and dreams don't always shield you from the cruel reality of never having enough. Despite their tireless efforts, poverty lingered like an unwelcome guest, always taking more than it gave.

My mother breastfed Wilfrid until he was two, knowing it was his best chance at nourishment. However, soon after Wilfrid was weaned from breast feeding, he changed. His hair turned orange, his belly swelled, his skin grew shiny, and he suffered from frequent bouts of diarrhea. My parents were terrified, but they had no money to take him to a doctor. In our village, sickness after weaning was often blamed on *vole lèt*—the belief that if a child nurses after weaning, the milk becomes poisonous. Desperation and fear fed this myth, and people pointed to it as the cause of Wilfrid's illness.

Just six months after he was weaned, at two and a half years old, Wilfrid died in their arms. My parents' heartbreak was immeasurable. They became part of a grim statistic—one in twelve children in Haiti dies before the age of five.[1]

Of course, Wilfrid didn't die because of vole lèt. He died of *kwashiorkor*—severe protein malnutrition, a silent killer that preys on children during the fragile window after weaning. His orange hair, bloated belly, and swollen limbs were all textbook signs. But textbooks don't exist in places like ours. Poverty left no space for medical advice, only myths and prayers. And for my family, it left a hole that would never be filled.

The loss of their firstborn was a devastating blow that shook my parents to their core. It was a grief so profound, and it tested their strength and resilience in unimaginable ways. Life was already a daily battle, but this loss cut deeper than anything they had faced before.

Gratitude became their lifeline. They believed that regardless of the circumstances, God always gives reasons to be thankful. In every hardship, they searched for His hand—trusting that even in the darkest moments, there was something to give thanks for.

---

[1] "Health: Good Health for All Children." UNICEF. Accessed August 21, 2025. https://www.unicef.org/haiti/en/node/251.

My parents held on to hope, trusting in God's plan, and they were blessed with more children to fill their lives with joy.

In 1970, Beatrice arrived—a beautiful, lively addition to the family. Two years later, Sandra joined them, and another two years after that, Pidens was born—each child adding more love and laughter to their home.

With the birth of their fourth child, my parents' dream of a wedding became impossible to ignore. Although money was still a hindrance in making this big day possible, each new life they brought into the world deepened their love and solidified their partnership, and the absence of a formal union weighed on their hearts. Poverty had always dictated what they could and couldn't do, but they refused to let it overshadow this important step.

After Pidens was born, they knew in their hearts it was time to get married. They couldn't wait for perfect circumstances or an extravagant celebration. What they longed for wasn't luxury, but the sacred act of standing before God and their loved ones to declare their unwavering commitment.

On March 23, 1975, with the love and support of friends and family, my parents finally made their dream of getting married a reality. They didn't have much, but they had each other—and a lot of determination. The pastor of their church, clearly moved by their story (and maybe their persistence), gifted them the wedding rings and set the ceremony for the crack of dawn—5 a.m. on a Sunday morning.

After exchanging vows in front of more than a hundred groggy but supportive guests, my parents decided to take things to the next level—literally. Without skipping a beat, they chose to be baptized right there, still dressed in their wedding clothes. Picture my mom in her simple white wedding dress and my dad in his humble suit, stepping into the water, their faces shining with joy and a touch of exhaustion.

The celebration afterward was as humble and heartfelt as they were. No grand reception, no towering wedding cake—just bread and cola shared with loved ones, served with smiles and laughter. It wasn't fancy, but it was perfect, a pure reflection of their love.

Every two years after that, like clockwork, my parents welcomed a new child into their growing family. Kateline, affectionately known as "Keke," arrived in 1978, bringing her lively spirit into the fold. I followed in 1980, and soon after came Isaac and then Farah, each one adding their own unique joy and chaos to the mix.

Then there was Melissa, whom we nicknamed "Camisha"—she decided the "two-year plan" wasn't for her and made her grand entrance nine years later, claiming the title of the youngest addition to the family.

Each child was a precious gift for my parents, a spark of light in a life where hope often felt elusive. Through every hardship and challenge, we were reminders that love and perseverance could overcome almost anything, one child and one joyful moment at a time.

CHAPTER 3
Something's Gotta Change

WHILE MY FAMILY found joy in each other, love, hope, and determination were not enough to shield us from hunger and the relentless grip of poverty. Sickness lay in wait, lurking like a shadow we could never quite escape.

I vividly remember one day when my brother Pidens was struck with typhoid fever. He was in unbearable pain, his cries cutting through the silence of our home like a blade. In our village, and even more so in my family, caring for the sick was a sacred duty. Money was always scarce, but when illness struck, the entire community would rally together. They'd extend lines of credit, ensuring food was available to help nurse the sick back to health.

I can still see him lying there, writhing in agony, surrounded by plates of nourishing food meant to restore his strength. Yet, while he had enough to eat, the rest of us survived on scraps. I was only ten years old, but the memory is burned into my mind. I remember wishing, with every ounce of my being, that I could trade places with him. As selfish as this sounds—if it meant having access to that food, I was willing to endure the sickness, the pain—anything to escape the gnawing hunger that never left my belly. It was a moment that shaped me, a moment when I realized the depths of both love and desperation that come with poverty. Even as a child, I knew what it meant to sacrifice, to hope, and to ache for a life where survival wasn't a daily battle.

My younger sister Farah was also often sick as a child, and when they had the money, my mom and papa spent countless days taking her to the doctor for help. She suffered from seizures and eye problems, and every visit brought back memories of losing their firstborn, Wilfrid. They were determined not to lose another child if it was within their power, but sometimes, due to lack of money, Farah simply stayed home sick. My niece, Cherline, Beatrice's daughter, who was just nine months apart from Farah, was also often sick.

Every bout of illness demanded money my parents didn't possess. They had goats and chickens, which they sold to pay for medical bills and doctor's visits. When there was nothing left to sell, my parents were terrified the girls would die before their fifth birthdays. They couldn't bear that thought, being part of the statistic one more time.

My family had to face a harsh reality—what we were doing wasn't enough. I could feel it in my mama's sighs at the end of a long day. She had a dream for us, her children—education and a life free from poverty. I remember her saying with quiet conviction, "Our life is not the life I want for my children." Those words still echo in my mind.

My mother's dream became her driving force. She refused to let us inherit her struggles. Every day, she worked tirelessly, her determination so fierce that it left no room for excuses. I saw it in the way she rose before the sun each day, her hands rough from years of labor. She was willing to do whatever it took to ensure we wouldn't end up like her.

My father shared the same resolve. Sacrifices were abundant—meals were skipped, and rest was forfeited. I often overheard their late-night conversations about our future. Their voices were low but intense, filled with hope, fear, and strategy. They possessed little beyond their faith and each other, but they knew they needed a way out, a plan that would offer their children new opportunities. Their conversations always circled back to one thing—education. They believed it was our only way forward, our only shot at breaking the cycle of poverty. United by a common vision, my parents prayed for God to show them a way.

They soon discovered an orphanage that had just opened its doors in the capital, Port-au-Prince. They learned it was started by someone from St. Michel named Gladys. Although the thought of placing their children in an orphanage was terrifying, they decided to inquire more about it. They had many difficult conversations with each other about this heart-wrenching decision but resisted the idea until one day, Farah became very sick. They had no money left for her care, and while Cherline's joyful, bubbling spirit lit up every room, behind her radiant smile, her health was also slipping away far too quickly.

In our village, adoption carried a heavy stigma. People looked at any family who adopted out their children with disdain and contempt, making them feel small and unworthy. It was a cruel and isolating experience. Yet, for my parents, the situation had reached a breaking point, and the decision became clearer with each passing day: If they did not give these girls up, they would not survive.

Farah and Cherline were inseparable, bound not only by blood but by the closeness of their ages and the life they shared. They did everything together—playing, laughing, and finding comfort in each other during the hardest moments. My parents couldn't imagine separating them. They knew that if only one of them were given up for adoption, it would shatter the other's heart. The pain of losing each other might be just as unbearable as the hardships they were already facing. And if Farah and Cherline had to leave, at least they could face the unknown together.

So, in the spring of 1989, poverty pushed my parents to an unthinkable edge—a place no parent should ever have to stand. With love and sorrow intertwined, they made the heart-wrenching and impossible choice to surrender Farah and Cherline—a choice they hoped would ultimately save the girls' lives.

Beatrice's heart broke knowing she could not provide for her little girl, her only child whom she loved with her whole heart, and my papa felt defeated—full of life and stamina to work yet living in a country that provided little opportunity to flourish. It was absolutely heartbreaking.

The night before the girls were to leave, my parents sat us down and said it would be our last night with our little sister and niece. My heart fractured under their words. I clung to them like my life depended on it, my fingers tracing the softness of their skin, committing every detail to memory—the curve of their tiny hands, the warmth of their breath, the sound of their giggles still lingering in the air. I had been their protector, their playmate, their guide. I taught them how to find the sweetest mangoes, how to chew sugar cane without cutting their lips, how to jump with joy in a game of hopscotch, and how to turn scraps of cloth into dolls. We were inseparable.

But now, I had to do the impossible—let them go.

I sobbed with a desperation that shook my bones, as if crying hard enough could somehow stop time or change fate. I begged heaven for a miracle, but by morning, they were gone. The house felt like a hollow shell, stripped of its heart. The silence wasn't just quiet—it was deafening, a void so loud it swallowed everything.

My mama had left early in the morning to take them 140 miles away to the orphanage in Port-au-Prince, riding a bus for over ten hours alone because they couldn't afford for my father to go with her. She readied herself to hand the girls over to strangers, trusting God to fill in the gaps where human love had no choice but to surrender.

When my mama finally returned to St. Michel, we begged her to tell us everything. We hung on every word, hoping for good news, but her story only offered anguish and despair.

Her voice cracked as she described how Farah and Cherline clung to her skirt, sobbing, "Please, Mommy, don't leave us. We'll be better kids. We won't cry when we're hungry—just don't leave us!" I could see the tears building in her eyes as she told us how the orphanage nanny had to pry their tiny hands from her skirt. My mama kept walking, her steps heavy as stone, their voices echoing behind her: "Mom ... Mommy ... Mommyyyyyy ..." Her heart didn't just break—it shattered into pieces that she would never fully put back together. She didn't look back—not because she didn't love them, but because if she had, she would have crumbled.

To this day, I still don't have words for that pain. It's a hollowing, a tearing, an immeasurable grief. It's knowing that love isn't always enough. It's realizing that poverty will make you sacrifice even the ones you swore you'd never lose.

We tried to move on, but their absence was a wound that never healed.

We prayed for kind nannies, for gentle hands to care for them, and for a future where they wouldn't feel abandoned. We pleaded for a good, godly family to adopt them both—so they would not be separated—and to love them as we did. But those prayers seemed to hang in the air.

We had no power to decide where they would go, who would call them "daughters" or "sisters," or what country would claim them as its own. The orphanage had ties to faraway places—names that felt more like distant planets than real destinations: the US, Canada, France, Australia, etc. We had sent them into the vast unknown, with nothing but hope to cling to, praying against all odds that they would land somewhere safe.

Then, the rumors began—whispers that children in orphanages were being sold for their organs or trafficked as slaves. Each rumor was a fresh cut, deeper than the last. My father, already broken with grief, reached his limit.

One night in May, a little more than two months after the girls were brought to the orphanage, my papa turned to my mama, his voice trembling, eyes hollow with despair. "Rose, please, let's go get our girls. We gave them up for a better life, but these rumors ... they will kill our girls, Rose. Please, let's bring them back."

His words ignited a fire in my mama, and they began saving every coin they could scrape together. After two months of toil and sacrifice, my mama set off for Port-au-Prince alone once more. She rode the same crowded bus, 140 miles of uncertainty pounding in her chest. This time, she was going to bring them home.

But when she arrived at the orphanage, her world crumbled. "They're gone," the staff said flatly. Her breath caught in her throat. "The girls have been placed with a family," they told her.

On June 22, 1989, Farah and Cherline, only three-and-a-half and three years old at the time, left for the United States.

Gone. Just like that. No goodbyes. No second chances. Gone.

Their departure left us with a flood of unanswered questions: Would they ever remember us as their family? Where in the world were they now? Were they happy? Would they ever think of us or remember us? Did they feel abandoned? Did they feel loved? The questions were endless and painfully so, haunting us with no answers in sight.

All that was left to do was surrender them to God. My parents prayed for mercy, begging Him to place the girls in a home where they would be loved, cherished, and protected. But for my father, it was a wound too deep to heal. He blamed himself for waiting too long, for letting fear paralyze him, for not protecting his little girls. That regret never left him, and depression settled over him like a shadow that refused to move.

CHAPTER 4

Port-au-Prince

AFTER FARAH AND CHERLINE's adoption, life began to shift in quiet but significant ways. My oldest sister Beatrice settled in Cap-Haitien, and determined to keep our family moving forward, my mama began going back and forth to Port-au-Prince about three times a year to sell charcoal, vegetables, spices, and fiery scotch bonnet peppers. Summer was her busiest season, and she hustled to save enough for school fees for my older siblings. On these trips, she often stayed with her younger sister, Jesula—whom we lovingly called Mansé.

Sometimes, Mom would bring my sister Sandra along. For Sandra, these trips were more than a chore; they were an adventure just like when my papa used to visit the bourg when he was a kid. Port-au-Prince was a world away from St. Michel, and she soaked it all in—the bustle of the big city, the endless sights, and the thrill of helping Mom sell goods. Back in St. Michel, she would boast to her friends about her trips, weaving playful stories that made her sound like a city girl with grand tales to tell.

On one of these visits, my mama's sister, Mansé, made a suggestion: "Why not let Sandra stay with us and go to school here?" she proposed. Port-au-Prince had public schools with resources that St. Michel couldn't offer. Sandra's eyes lit up at the idea of living in the big city, and my mom saw it as a rare chance for something better. She spoke with my papa, and after careful thought, he agreed.

That fall, Sandra moved to Port-au-Prince and enrolled in a public school in Carrefour Pean. It was a fresh start—a door opened by the hands of family and much prayer. What began as a humble effort to sell goods on the streets had blossomed into a new chapter for Sandra—a chance to dream bigger, reach higher, and see possibilities beyond the borders of St. Michel. Even though the journey was long and exhausting, Mom frequently traveled to see Sandra, bringing food and selling goods to support our family, balancing her role as a mother, a provider, and a woman with unyielding hope.

One fateful trip turned out to be more than she bargained for. As her bus climbed a rain-slicked hill, the road gave way, sending it plummeting seventy feet into a ravine. Miraculously, my mama, seated on the roof, was caught by a tree branch and left dangling above the wreckage. Below, screams and lifeless bodies filled the hillside.

Onlookers rushed to help and were stunned by her survival. One man, in disbelief, said, "Stay there—I need to get a journalist!" As they waited, villagers brought her food and water, treating her like a living miracle.

Meanwhile, news of the crash reached St. Michel. My mama's younger brother, Tayan, along with my papa, searched the morgue, but when they didn't find her, our family assumed the worst. Funeral preparations began—white curtains were hung, coffee was brewed, and mourners gathered.

I cried myself to sleep every night. The pain was crushing—so heavy it felt like it could swallow me whole. My heart pounded in my chest with fear and disbelief, and I kept wondering, *How will I survive without my mom?* The thought of life without her was too much to bear.

Days later, my mama walked into her own funeral! Grief turned to shock, then utter joy, as people wept and praised God for what they believed was a miracle. I was overjoyed—my hands trembled as I touched every inch of her, needing to make sure she was real, that she wasn't a ghost, and that my mind wasn't playing tricks on me. I cried harder than I ever had that day, but those tears were different. They were tears of joy—tears of hope restored, of love returned. I thanked God fervently for giving her back to us.

Her survival became a legendary tale, whispered with awe across the village, a living testimony of grace and the power of prayer. And even after that harrowing experience, she didn't stop making the journey. No hardship—not even death itself—could keep her from providing for her children.

Each time my mama returned from Port-au-Prince, she was even more determined to create a better life for us. She saw opportunities in the city that didn't exist in St. Michel, where poverty held us captive. Working in the capital brought financial relief, and watching my sister Sandra thrive—despite her heavy chores—gave my mama hope that the city could offer a brighter future.

One day, Mama told my papa she needed to move permanently to Port-au-Prince to find steady work. She would send money for our school fees while he provided for our daily needs. He resisted at first, fearing what her absence would do to our family, but he knew she was right. St. Michel offered no future. With a heavy heart, he gave her his blessing.

When she told us she would leave in a week and could only visit once a year, we were devastated. I was just nine years old, too young to understand. Her absence felt like losing a part of ourselves. She had been our anchor—the one who cooked, braided our hair, and pressed our clothes. Without her, our home felt empty.

In late 1989, my mama left for Port-au-Prince.

There, my mama stayed with a childhood friend from St. Michel, sharing a cramped one-room house already crowded with eight people. Her decision to stay there was strategic—the location was close to a potential job opportunity. But living in Port-au-Prince was nothing like her previous visits. The city was loud, fast, and unrelenting. Finding work was harder than she imagined.

Much like the little girl who once asked for work at the deputy's house, my mom did what she'd always done—she knocked on doors. Walking from house to house, she asked strangers if they needed help. Eventually, she found temporary work as a laundry worker. The job was grueling. She washed piles of clothes by hand and carried heavy jugs of water on her head every day. She left at dawn and returned late at night, her body aching, but it was something—at least for now.

After a few months of living with her friend, she was informed that she had just two weeks to leave, as someone else would be moving into the small house. Panic crept in. She thought about asking her sister Mansé for a place to stay, but she knew her sister's tiny home was already far too cramped. Every passing day brought more anxiety, and by Thursday—just two days before her deadline—she felt completely lost. Overwhelmed with fear and uncertainty, she prayed to Jehovah Jireh, God our Provider, and cried herself to sleep.

That night, she had a dream. In it, a man held two cups—one filled with oil, the other with water. He poured the oil over her head. Shocked, she protested, "Why did you pour oil on me? I have no clothes to change into!" But the man calmly replied, "Go to Gladys and ask her for a job."

Gladys not only started the orphanage that was home to Farah and Cherline before they were adopted to the United States, but she was also a prominent businesswoman in Port-au-Prince. She oversaw a large nonprofit that managed hospitals, schools, and orphanages. When my mom first arrived in the city, she had visited Gladys in search of a job. Though there were no openings at the time, Gladys encouraged her to stay close in case an opportunity arose. This glimmer of hope played a role in my mom's decision to stay with her childhood friend.

When she woke up, she shared the dream with her host. They both felt the presence of the Holy Spirit and prayed for clarity and courage. Convinced the dream was a sign from God, Mom decided to act. She didn't know Gladys' exact address but had a rough idea of the area. She asked around until someone finally directed her to Gladys' residence.

When she arrived at the gate, Gladys happened to be outside. Their eyes met.

"Are you Farah's mom?" Gladys asked.

My mom said, "*Wi*." ("Yes")

"God has sent you. Come in."

Gladys revealed that she had forgotten about Mom and was about to hire someone else for an opening. "I'm so glad you came," she said. It was as if the dream had led Mom to the very moment she was supposed to be in. She was hired that same day—a Friday. With just twenty-four hours left to vacate her temporary home, divine intervention had come right on time.

Back at her childhood friend's house, she gathered her belongings, her heart overflowing with gratitude. Her new role would be a housekeeper at a missionary's home, working directly under Gladys' supervision.

Her first day was unforgettable. Gladys took her on a tour of the house that felt like a palace to Mom. The garden was lush and manicured, and the house had beautiful architecture and character. For someone who had only known dirt floors and shared sleeping spaces, other than the deputy's home, it was like stepping into a dream. Room by room, Gladys showed her the living room, kitchen, and bedrooms. Finally, she led her to a modest but clean room in the back. It had a twin bed and a simple dresser, and the floor was tiled. Mom admired it, thinking it was for another guest.

At the end of the tour, she asked, "Where will I sleep?"

Gladys smiled. "That last room I showed you—it's yours."

Mom couldn't believe it. Her whole life, she never had a room of her own with a dresser and a table. It felt surreal. Her excitement was so overwhelming that she accidentally locked herself out of the room that very day.

The pay was modest—175 gourdes per month, roughly $25 at the time—but missionaries would sometimes leave her generous tips, which made all the difference. Determined to make the most of this new opportunity, Mom devised a plan with my sister Sandra. They dreamed of building a small house in Port-au-Prince and bringing the rest of the family from St. Michel to live with them.

The plan was bold, but so was my mom. She found a small plot of land on Rue Amazon in Faustin 1er. Owning land felt like an impossible dream, especially with her modest wages, but she had learned how to make the impossible possible.

She joined a *sol*—a community savings group. A sol works like this: A group of people contributes a fixed amount of money into a communal pot each month. Every month, one member of the group receives the full amount from the pot. It's a system built on trust, discipline, and patience. By participating in the sol and saving the tips she received from the missionaries, Mom slowly gathered enough money to buy the plot of land. It wasn't easy, but she didn't stop. She knew that owning land would change everything for our family. Month by month, she worked toward this dream.

However, life in St. Michel only grew harder with her gone. Each day became a struggle to stretch what little we had. Mom had always been incredibly resourceful—washing clothes by hand, cooking flavorful meals from meager ingredients, tending to our school needs, and doing everything she could to keep us grounded and hopeful. Without her, the house felt hollow. A heavy silence settled over everything. We missed her presence, her guidance, the warmth of her voice. Even the sunniest days felt uncertain. Her absence was a constant reminder of just how much our world depended on her strength.

Although my papa was a skilled carpenter and tin roofer, he struggled to find work. His daily earnings determined whether we ate, but opportunities were scarce. Frustration and shame weighed on him, and though he never spoke of it, his despair ran deep. At the age of eighteen, I found out just how severe Dad's depression was when he attempted suicide.

Mom's annual visit was the brightest light in our year. For 358 long days, we felt her absence like an ache, counting down to the one week when her warmth and laughter would fill our home again. When she finally arrived, everything felt whole and safe. Her summer visit meant everything to us.

She always came with gifts—not just hugs and love but little treasures that felt like magic: new outfits, fresh socks and underwear, things we needed but rarely had. And then there were the treats—delights we could only dream about when she wasn't there. She'd bring slices of soft bread and muffins, sweet and rare—we savored slowly, not knowing when we'd taste them again—and hard candy, each piece feeling like a small miracle. These gifts from her world made us feel special, like we were part of the city life she described.

Going to places like the maché with my mother made me feel like I belonged to something bigger. Walking beside her, I was proud—she knew everyone, greeting each by name, asking about their families, remembering every detail. A quick walk stretched into more than an hour as she stopped to talk with everyone we passed, offering her warmth and kindness.

I'd follow her closely, playing a game of stepping into her foot-prints on the dusty road, trying to match her stride. Each step felt like I was borrowing a piece of her strength and courage, like I was walking in her spirit. I felt proud to be her child, hoping one day to carry myself with the same grace and elegance.

But all too soon, the week would slip away, and the goodbye was like tearing a piece of my heart. Watching her leave was always the hardest part, knowing that her warm presence, the treats, and the regular meals would end, and we'd go back to the daily struggle. As we waved, I felt a deep sadness, already missing her before she was even gone.

Mom was always sad when it was time for her to leave, too. She would gather all of us together, her voice soft but full of purpose, explaining why she had to make the sacrifices that kept her away from us. "I'm doing this for you," she would say, her eyes welling with tears, the depth of her love and responsibility displayed on her face.

Despite the ache, we began to understand her sacrifice. Every day she was away, she was working for us, for a future she dreamed we'd have. Her conviction, inner strength, and willingness to act on signs and dreams from God had brought her this far, and giving up was not an option. This was the beginning of a new chapter for all of us. Her love, her stories, and her hugs were like a bridge to a brighter tomorrow, carrying us through the year until she could be with us again. Her visits reminded us that we were never truly apart because her heart was always with us, just as ours were with her, bound by a shared hope and love that no distance could break.

CHAPTER 5

The Power of the Uniform

ONE DAY, WHEN I was ten, shortly after the girls were adopted and Mom had moved to Port-au-Prince, my parents told me I would be starting school! This was far later than most students in St. Michel who began at three years old, but preschool and kindergarten were out of reach for my family—my parents simply couldn't afford it.

As the financial strain on my family had deepened over the years, so had my longing to be like the other students—to have a uniform, a teacher, and a place to belong. Each day I waited, the ache grew stronger. I wanted to be seen, to be counted, to feel like I belonged to something bigger than the walls of our hut. For years, I watched students my age walk past our house each morning, hand-in-hand with their classmates, their laughter echoing in the air. I sat in front of the house in the dust, watching them disappear down the road, wondering when it would be my turn. The wait felt like forever, but after seven long years, it was finally here.

As I got older, I began to understand that education is more than learning; it's a pathway to dignity and opportunity. For children in poverty, it's their greatest hope. It transforms "I have no life" into "I have a future." Poverty tries to tell you that you don't matter, that your voice doesn't count. It makes you believe that being destitute is your destiny. But education pushes back. It gives you words, confidence, and the power to be seen and heard. This is why education matters—it doesn't just change lives; it breaks cycles and reclaims futures.

Being so young, I didn't understand all of this. I just knew that school was where you learned, where you met friends, and where life could be different. And I had already started dreaming of becoming a nurse.

In St. Michel, nurses weren't just healthcare workers—they were guardians, protectors, and trusted figures who carried hope in their hands. Doctors were rare, but nurses were present. They bandaged wounds, delivered babies, comforted grieving families, and eased suffering. They were everything our community could count on, and I wanted to be that kind of strength—the person others turned to in their most vulnerable moments. I knew that school was the only way to get there.

I remember so clearly the moment my parents told me. It felt like the whole world had shifted. My heart leapt in my chest. I was so overwhelmed with joy I could barely stand still.

I'll never forget getting ready for that first week of school. I could hardly sleep at night. My mind spun with excitement and nerves. *Will I make friends? Will they like me?* My mama came back to St. Michel from Port-au-Prince to witness my first few days of school. The night before my first day, my mama prepared everything like she was handling something sacred. She ironed my blue and white pleated uniform with care, smoothing out every wrinkle as if each crease were an obstacle to hope. She polished my little black shoes until they sparkled, and she lay out my socks, barrettes, and ribbons like treasures. I watched her with wide eyes, my heart swelling with pride and gratitude.

That night, I barely closed my eyes. *How could I sleep when the dream I had clung to for so long was finally coming true?* I lay awake imagining myself walking to school like the other students I had watched for years. But this time, I wouldn't be watching. I would be one of them. I would have a teacher who called my name. I would have classmates to walk beside me. I would belong.

That first day of school was more than the start of my education—it was the first time I felt like I had a chance to change my story. For so long, it felt like life was something that happened to other people, something I could only witness from a distance. But stepping into that classroom, dressed in my new uniform with shoes that shone, I knew something was different. I was part of something bigger. I was seen. I was counted.

I'll never forget the feeling of putting on my school uniform. It was like stepping into a suit of armor—transformative and powerful. That blue and white uniform made me feel like I belonged to something greater than myself. It wasn't just fabric. Hope was stitched into every seam. Poverty made everything feel uncertain, but my uniform was a promise that I was moving toward something better.

The walk to school was a twenty-minute journey along a dusty dirt road. It was always an adventure. The road shifted with the weather. When it was dry, it was coated in thick, powdery dust that clung to our skin, hair, and uniforms. By the time I reached school, my shoes were covered in a layer of brown dust, and my feet felt gritty inside them. When it rained, that same road became a muddy obstacle course, swallowing our feet with each step. After a while, my shoes became cracked and worn from use; they barely held together. The soles were so thin I could feel the sharp edges of rocks beneath my feet. Sometimes, I'd fold the flapping sole back into place and keep walking, pretending it wasn't a problem.

But I didn't walk alone. As I walked with my older siblings, other children from the village joined us, forming little groups that grew with each turn. One of the most beautiful sights on that walk was the sea of children in uniforms. Each school had its own colors and design, turning the streets into a mosaic of blues, greens, yellows, and whites. It was like a living tapestry of hope. I loved seeing the variety of uniforms and guessing which schools they belonged to. Each child wearing one carried the sense of pride that I felt, too. On the way, we talked, laughed, and shared dreams. We dreamed of being doctors, nurses, teachers—anything that sounded bigger than the life we knew. Our dreams felt unstoppable in our uniforms, on that road.

HARSH REALITY

Our house didn't have an alarm clock. Instead, we woke to the calls of roosters perched in the tall trees around our hut. At exactly 5:50 a.m., the first one would crow, and by 6 a.m., it was a full-blown symphony. Their call was impossible to ignore—a natural alarm that signaled it was time to start the day.

Mornings followed a strict routine. My siblings and I emptied our chamber pots and brushed our teeth. If we had food that day, I'd help prepare breakfast. On good days, we'd have boiled plantains with herring sauce. On other days, we left for school with empty bellies, hoping there would be something to eat later.

I soon learned that school life wasn't all joy. Discipline was harsh. Corporal punishment was common and accepted by parents, teachers, and school administrations. I'll never forget one day in fourth grade when my teacher, who was also my pastor, called me to the board for a *dictée* (dictation). I knew I was a good student, but as soon as he called my name, fear rushed in. I missed the final "s" on "*Vous* êtes" ("you are"), and that mistake cost me. Each time I wrote it incorrectly, I felt the sharp sting of a lash on my back. Ten lashes later, with tears in my eyes, I finally wrote it correctly. I promised myself that day that if I ever became a teacher, I would never treat a student that way.

Even church was a form of discipline. Because our school was housed in a church, Sunday service wasn't optional. We were required to attend Sunday school at 7:30 a.m., followed by a service that often lasted until noon. Skipping church wasn't an option. If you did, lashes followed on Monday at school. For many of us, this taught us to see God as a figure of punishment rather than love. But deep down I knew He was a lovely and compassionate God.

One of my favorite parts of school was the cafeteria. It wasn't much—just wheat and green beans every day—but for me, it was everything. At 11 a.m., I knew I would get a meal. Some days, it was the only meal I'd have. If I left for school with an empty belly and returned home to find no dinner, I clung to that one meal at school as if it were gold. It filled more than just my stomach—it gave me something to look forward to.

But there were days when my dream of education collided with the harsh reality of poverty.

Fifth grade. I'll never forget it. The principal called me out of class. I thought maybe I was in trouble, which happened more often than not, unfortunately. But it was worse than that. I was told I couldn't stay in school because my parents owed 100 gourdes—barely one US dollar. One dollar! I stood there frozen, hoping he was joking. But he wasn't. *"Ale lakay ou."* "Go home," he said. Those two words hit me harder than any lash ever could. Go home? Over 100 gourdes? It felt like a cruel joke, but it wasn't.

With humiliation, I walked back to my classroom and gathered my belongings with all my classmates watching my every move. The embarrassment I felt was unbearable. Everyone knew why a student was called out during school hours, and it felt like my dreams were slipping away.

I walked home that day in silence, my head down, my uniform suddenly feeling heavy on my back. The road I had walked with so much pride now felt endless. My mind replayed the moment over and over. *One hundred gourdes. Just one hundred gourdes.* My shoes, already falling apart, dragged along the dirt. With every step, I felt the broken sole flap against the ground like it was mocking me. I didn't cry—not at first. I held it in, hoping I could push it down. But by the time I got home, I couldn't hold it anymore. I sat on the ground and cried so hard my chest ached.

The next morning, I watched my friends walk past my house wearing their uniforms. The same friends I used to walk with, laugh with, and share stories with on the road to school. I watched them walk away, and I stayed behind. It felt like being forgotten while the world moved on without me.

I couldn't bear sitting at home while my future slipped away. I took matters into my own hands. I visited a nearby farm, gathered sweet oranges, and filled a bucket before heading to the school grounds to sell them. Despite the ridicule from some students—who mocked me and asked if I was ashamed to be selling produce instead of attending school—I refused to let their words deter me. I was determined to pursue my education, no matter the obstacles. I repeated this effort multiple times each day, earning a few pennies that I proudly gave to my parents to contribute to my tuition. Nothing was going to stand in the way of me going back to school.

Ten days. That's how long I stayed home, watching my dream slip further from reach. My parents did everything they could to gather the 100 gourdes. They sold what they could, skipped meals, and worked nonstop. After two long weeks, they finally had enough to pay the fee, and I was allowed back in school.

But something had changed in me.

Even though I was back, the fear of being sent home again never left. I sat in class with my heart on edge, always waiting for the principal to call my name. My love for learning was still there, but my belief in the dream had dimmed. I realized something: Dreams are dangerous when they can be taken from you so easily.

That was the day I tried to stop dreaming. Not because I didn't want to, but because I was afraid to. I told myself, *Don't dream too big, Miquette. Dreams hurt too much when they break.*

But something inside me refused to die. I didn't know it then, but that little spark was still there. It didn't matter how dim it was—it was there. The voice that poverty had tried to silence was simply whispering, fragile and unsure, afraid to hope again.

Even now, I think about that little girl in her blue and white uniform. She didn't have much—no food, no money, no comfort—but she still had hope. She knew that every morning she put on that uniform, she was defying the odds. She was claiming a future that wasn't promised, but that she believed in anyway. That belief, and the audacity to dream big, is what kept her going.

CHAPTER 6

Between the Well and Home

EVEN THOUGH I had started school, I still had many chores to do. In my village, chores were a way of life. They taught us discipline, patience, and pride in the little we had. And cleanliness wasn't optional; it was a reflection of who you were. Every morning began with one simple rule: "Brush your teeth before you speak." No toothpaste? No problem. We had baking soda, and when things were tight, charcoal. Scrubbing your teeth with burnt wood was humbling, but it got the job done.

Once we were "clean" by village standards, it was time for work. First up, we gathered our "beds"—a pile of worn rags we slept on—and swept the dirt floor of our hut. Sweeping dirt might sound pointless, but it wasn't. We'd sprinkle water on it to keep the dust down, and somehow, it felt fresh. Then, we'd head outside to sweep the path in front of our home. It wasn't just about appearances; it was about pride. We wanted everyone passing by to know that, even if we had little, we still had dignity.

Water collection was next, and it was no small task. Water—the most basic necessity for human survival—was a luxury. Can you imagine that? Something so fundamental, something most people take for granted, was a daily struggle for us.

There were two wells within walking distance of my house, about a fifteen-minute trek away. My friends and sister Keke made several trips throughout the day, ensuring we had enough water to sustain our household. Every morning, before getting ready for school, we'd set out with our empty buckets, and after school, we'd do it all over again. The water we collected was used for drinking, cooking, and washing—each drop precious, each spill a quiet loss.

Despite the effort, I often enjoyed the task. There was never a dull moment at the well. It was more than a place to fetch water; it was where we caught up on town gossip, debated the latest scandals, and sometimes, witnessed full-blown arguments over who had cursed whom with an evil spirit. The well was a community hub, a space where life unfolded in ways both lighthearted and dramatic.

Because of our circumstances, my parents had no choice but to leave home most days in search of work, which meant I had more freedom than any teenager should. They did their best to instill in me and my siblings a sense of responsibility, including abstinence, good manners, and another rule: Never engage in a fistfight—no matter what. But trips to the well were like *The Hunger Games: Village Edition*. You had to be sharp, fast, and ready for anything.

With no one watching over me, I had to toughen up fast. Self-defense wasn't just a useful skill—it was survival. Fighting was an everyday occurrence in my neighborhood, and fights at the well were as common as mosquitoes—some I walked into, some found me, and a few I definitely should have walked away from. I had a reputation: the kind of nice girl who didn't start fights but never backed down from one. And, for better or worse, I rarely lost. Certainly not the legacy I intended to leave!

It would have been much nicer to be known as the girl who helped frail, elderly women carry their buckets of water.

I still remember one fight I started because I was certain I'd win. Spoiler alert: I didn't. I walked away with bruises on my body and my pride abandoned at the well—probably still sitting there, laughing at me.

That day, I made a life-altering decision: no more starting fights.

I wish I could say it was because I always got a big spanking at home when my parents found out, or that I had grown wiser and more mature. But the truth? I stopped because I got my behind handed to me.

From then on, I chose peace.

I'm grateful for the friends who helped make those grueling trips to and from the well more bearable. My walks with Vida became sacred spaces where we dared to dream. Vida dreamed of becoming a doctor in the same way I dreamed of becoming a nurse. We used to joke that one day we'd be so successful and busy saving the world, we'd pay people to carry those buckets for us. The dreams didn't make the buckets any lighter, but they made the journey feel less burdensome. Of course, how those dreams would ever come true, we had no idea.

When the dry season came, the routine turned into a grueling ordeal. Water became scarce, and access was no longer guaranteed. Most wells belonged to private owners, and getting permission to use them was unpredictable. Many times, we knocked on doors only to be turned away and forced to return home empty-handed. Other times, we walked for hours under the blazing sun, searching for any source of water as if we were on a treasure hunt—only the reward wasn't gold.

When we finally found a well, relief washed over us. The moment was exhilarating, but the challenge was far from over. I'd balance a five-gallon bucket on my head, clutch a two-gallon jug in each of my hands, and begin the long trek home. Each step required patience, balance, and sheer determination. Spill a drop, and it felt like a personal failure. Water wasn't just life—it was everything.

Can you imagine not having a single drop of water in your home? No water for drinking, for cooking, for bathing? That was my reality too many times. Some days, I had barely enough water to dampen a towel for a makeshift bath. I became an expert in rationing—learning which parts of my body to wash first, based on the precious ounces of water available.

I lived in constant fear that my classmates would notice. The days I couldn't properly bathe were the hardest. Without deodorant, without even soap sometimes, I could feel their stares lingering on me. They didn't have to say the words—I saw the judgment in their eyes, the wrinkled noses, the turned faces. The unspoken message was loud enough: You stink.

And in those moments, I wanted to disappear.

SATURDAYS, SUMMERS, AND NEW YEARS

With no running water, plumbing, or electricity, over 95 percent of St. Michel's residents rely on a nearby river for their most basic needs (a reality they still face today). Saturday is *jounen lesiv*—washing day—the busiest day of the week. Washing clothes in the river is backbreaking work. It is also a ritual, a gathering, a moment of connection—but only because we had no other choice.

During the week, only a few trickled down to scrub their garments, but on Saturdays, the river came alive. Women and children filled the banks, their laughter and voices blending with the rhythmic slap of fabric against smooth stones. It was always women—mothers, daughters, aunts, grandmothers—rarely men. The river wasn't just a place for chores; it was a lifeline, a space where burdens felt lighter when shared.

I started going to the river with my mom and sisters as far back as I can remember. By the time I was seven, I was already washing some of my own clothes. At nine, when my mama moved to the city and my older siblings dispersed to places like Cap-Haitien and Gonaïves, it was just Keke, my little brother Isaac, my father, and me. That's when Keke and I had to take over completely. While other children played, we spent our Saturdays at the river, scrubbing dirt and sweat from our few sets of clothes and the sheets we slept on each night.

Every Saturday, Keke and I woke before dawn, hoping to finish while the sun was still high. We gathered the pile of clothes, stuffed them into a *kivet* (bucket), balanced the heavy load on our heads, and walked an hour to the river. My neck ached, and my arms burned, but there was no alternative. It was responsibility and duty.

I tried to find joy where I could. Keke, my friends, Vida, Anouse, and Edeline, and I planned all week for jounen lesiv, deciding what we would cook for lunch. It was the only part of the day that felt like a choice. After scrubbing and rinsing our clothes in the river, we lay them on the large, sunbaked rocks to dry. In the meantime, we built a fire—three stones and a handful of sticks—and cooked our meal. Some days, we made grits; other times, porridge or boiled plantains. Simple, but enough to keep us going.

Only after eating did we allow ourselves to be children again. We jumped into the river, letting the cool water wash away the sweat and exhaustion, stealing a few moments of laughter before our responsibilities reclaimed us. Drying the clothes took two to three hours, depending on the sun's heat. Saturdays should have been spent playing freely, but instead, we just had a brief intermission in a long day of labor.

I loved hearing the women sing as they washed, their voices carrying over the rushing water—songs of joy, struggle, and resilience. But regardless of the moments of connection, the work was relentless. Rain was our greatest enemy. Without the sun, our freshly washed clothes would stay damp, forcing us to haul them home, the kivet digging into our foreheads, each step more grueling than the last.

There was little room for childhood in poverty. While other children played, we carried buckets heavier than our small frames should have allowed. While they ran freely, we walked miles and did labor that was never meant for us. But in the village, age didn't matter. You did what had to be done.

Summer was my favorite time of the year. With no school and the freedom to roam, the season felt limitless. Our days were filled with joy and creativity. Without toys, I relied on resourcefulness to fill my days. Our humble hut was a place to sleep, not to live. Life happened outside, under vast blue skies that stretched endlessly with the promise of adventure.

Early on, I became an entrepreneur, determined to help my family. My first business was selling *fritay*—fried treats like marinade and *banan pézé* (fried plantains). Armed with 5 gourdes—barely a quarter—I set up shop in front of my house. Each sale filled me with pride as neighbors supported my small venture, reminding me that even in hardship, community and kindness thrived.

In the afternoons, I joined my best friend, Anouse, to sell kerosene gas. We walked the streets, shouting, "Gas! Gas! Gas!" in unison. It wasn't just about making money—it was the thrill of working and dreaming together. We alternated sales, earning 15 or 30 cents in a good evening. Afterward, we'd sit together counting coins, sharing laughter and dreams of a better life that echoed through the quiet streets.

Before moving to Port-au-Prince, my older sister Sandra noticed my entrepreneurial streak. She entrusted me with her rice and beans business, a significant operation with an inventory worth over 2,000 gourdes. I felt like I held the world in my hands. Each day, I brought home earnings—300 gourdes here, 400 there—and Sandra rewarded me with small amounts, 5 to 10 gourdes, enough to make me feel independent and valued. Her trust fueled my determination.

When I wasn't selling fritay, gas, or rice and beans, I helped my *grann*—my grandmother—sell spices at the market. Her *panier*, a large woven basket brimming with green onions, garlic, parsley, and thyme, was her livelihood. She balanced the heavy load on her head each morning and walked miles to the maché, where she sat all day selling her goods. For all her labor, she earned the equivalent of just one US dollar. Her only day off was Sunday.

I loved spending time with Grann, even though she had very little patience with us kids. She was a phenomenal cook, and I always looked forward to Sundays, when we would go to her house—just a short walk from ours—knowing she'd prepare her best meal on that special day. Food was often scarce during the week, but Sunday at Grann's felt like a celebration.

When our chores were all taken care of, we had freedom to play to our heart's content though we had to be creative since we had no toys. We played games like hopscotch using rope made from tree fiber. We played *osselet*, a game played with goat knuckle bones we found left from the rich people who could afford goat meat, and *zikòs*. Zikòs was a mix of marbles and punishment—joy and pain intertwined. We'd dig a small hole in the ground and take turns throwing marbles, trying to land them in or near the hole. The winner got to hit the opponent's knuckles with a marble until their marble fell into the hole. The sting was sharp, but the laughter was louder.

"Miquette, this is a boy's game. Get away from it," my parents would scold. But their warnings only fueled my determination to prove I was just as tough. I played with the boys, my knuckles red and aching.

In the winter, we all looked forward to New Years. In Haiti, January first was more than just the start of a new year—it was our Independence Day and the most anticipated time of the year for children. Parents prepared their best meals, with pumpkin soup as the centerpiece, but for me, the highlight was visiting my *marraine* (godmother).

Like all the other children in the village, I'd join the long line of kids on New Year's Day to visit our godparents—a cherished Haitian tradition. My godmother, Claudette, was always the one I looked forward to seeing most. I lovingly called her Marraine, and she gave the best gifts every year. I could hardly wait to see her.

Claudette was remarkable in every way. She worked for some of the most important people in the country: She was the nanny to the president's children. Because of her role, she often traveled with the presidential crew and had the opportunity to visit places I had only dreamed of. To me, she was like someone out of a storybook—elegant, worldly, and deeply kind.

During the holidays, Marraine always returned to St. Michel to visit her family. And every year, she never forgot me. Most years, she would give me 100 gourdes—a fortune for a little girl who rarely had more than five to her name. That small gift always felt like a treasure, filling my heart.

Life in St. Michel was hard, but it was rich with lessons. Each challenge, each shared dream, and each moment under the open sky added layers to who I was becoming. It was daily survival *and* preparation for the journey ahead. And even in the smallest, hardest moments, hope took root, and dreams quietly flourished.

CHAPTER 7
Courage and Silence

I ONCE TRAVELED to Port-au-Prince with my mama to help her sell her spices. It was a rare and exciting experience. Then, when I was around twelve, my papa entrusted me with the freedom to travel to Port-au-Prince alone to visit my mom. For a child, it felt monumental—a mix of excitement, pride, and trepidation. My heart raced with the thrill of adventure, but I also knew it came with a weight of responsibility.

Although my papa had given me permission to go, the decision weighed heavily on him and my mom. They coordinated my arrival but still worried incessantly. Papa, strong and steady as he was, couldn't hide the tension in his face as he hugged me goodbye. *"Atansyon, Miquette."* "Be careful, Miquette," he would say, his voice low but firm. They worried constantly—especially because they had no way to communicate with each other or with me while I was on the road.

The first time I made the trip, the fear in my papa's eyes stayed with me the entire way. I could feel the enormity of the trust he had placed in me. Each bump and jolt of the bus felt like a test, and every stranger's face was a question mark. I clutched my small bag tightly, my heart pounding as I replayed my father's parting words in my mind.

At the other end of the journey, my mama paced anxiously, scanning the horizon for any sign of me. With no phone and no way to communicate with my papa, she had no idea exactly when I had left St. Michel or when I might arrive. All she could do was wait—restless yet hopeful, her heart caught between fear and faith, praying I would arrive safely.

When I finally reached Port-au-Prince and saw my mom, her relief was palpable. She pulled me into a tight embrace, tears brimming in her eyes. "*Mèsi, Jezi*," she whispered, thanking Jesus that I had arrived safely. It was in that moment I realized just how much my parents worried—not just about the journey but about the world and the risks they could not shield me from.

Even though I had visited Port-au-Prince once before with my mama to help her sell spices, traveling there by myself was an entirely different experience. It was my first time navigating the city on my own, and everything felt bigger, louder, and more intense. Coming from the quiet, power-less nights of St. Michel, one of the things that struck me most were the city lights. I was captivated by the glow of the street lamps lining the roads, the headlights weaving through traffic, and the flicker of lights in buildings that never seemed to sleep.

The honking cars, shouting vendors, and fast-moving crowds overwhelmed me at times, but there was something magical about it, too. I clutched my bag tightly, trying to stay alert and take it all in. The city pulsed with energy and possibility, but it also demanded courage. For the first time, I wasn't just observing—I was finding my way.

Growing up in St. Michel, the police had always filled me with a quiet terror. Their presence in the town square, especially their guns, would make my heart race and my palms sweat. I'd go out of my way to avoid even passing by the police station. It wasn't because of a traumatic encounter—there was no singular event that scarred me. It was something deeper, a fear that gripped me in ways I didn't fully understand.

When I arrived in Port-au-Prince, that familiar unease surged back, stronger than ever. There they were again—men with guns.

But this time, they weren't the local police I had grown up fearing. These were white men in khaki uniforms, their rifles held tight, almost as if they were pointing them at civilians—such an unsettling feeling.

After my initial solo visit to Port-au-Prince, I proved to my parents I was mature enough to visit more often. One trip, however, became unforgettable, though not in the way I'd hoped.

After spending time with my mom, she gave me money to bring back to my family, including funds for food and school fees. I carefully tucked it into my pocket before starting my journey back to St. Michel.

I took the bus from Port-au-Prince to Gonaïves, where I would switch to another bus to reach St. Michel. When I got off the bus in Gonaïves, I felt a man press close to me, his hand brushed against my side. Instantly I remembered people talking about thieves and pick pocketers, so I patted my pocket, and my heart dropped—the money Mom gave to me was gone.

I turned around and made eye contact with the thief—he knew I'd caught him. Without a second thought, he took off, and I, a thirteen-year-old girl, ran after this grown man. He weaved through narrow alleyways and corridors, but I didn't hesitate, my only thought fixed on getting that money back. Eventually, he ducked into a house. I stopped outside, not daring to enter but determined not to let him think I'd give up.

Standing there, I began to cry, calling out to him, pleading for my money. A group of men nearby, playing dominoes, watched the scene unfold, listening as I told the thief that this was my school money, my bus fare—everything we had. The thief taunted me from inside, challenging me to come in, but I refused, telling him I would wait outside for as long as it took. Eventually, the men playing dominoes began urging him to return the money, but he ignored them. Finally, one of them, moved by my persistence, walked into the house and then came back out with my money.

"Little girl, you are a brave one," said the man who went to get my money.

"Go on, now," he said, handing me the money.

That moment stuck with me—the fear, the defiance, the help from strangers. Looking back, it feels surreal, a reminder of both the dangers I faced and the strength I found. At that age, I didn't think of risk; all I knew was that I couldn't go home without what I'd been trusted to bring. It was my determination, but also the kindness of strangers, that saved the day.

From then on, the journey to Port-au-Prince became more than just a trip to see my mama—it was a testament to the courage I didn't yet know I had. Little did I know, the experience of chasing down that thief and reclaiming what was rightfully mine prepared me to endure far more painful things in my teenage years.

Another task that I was responsible for growing up was going to the maché. Mondays and Fridays were my favorite days of the week because the maché came alive with vendors from all the surrounding communities. They filled every corner with everything from chickens and spices to fresh vegetables and fruit. These were the best days to bargain, as prices were typically lower than on other days of the week. The variety was unmatched, offering a chance to find items that weren't available on other days. It was our version of Black Friday—but instead of once a year, it happened twice a week.

On those days, my mama or father would hand me a list and a few coins with instructions to buy plantains, sweet potatoes, spinach, oil, leeks, tomato paste, and beans—all the essentials we needed to prepare the day's meals. The hustle and energy of the maché, paired with the thrill of finding the best deals, made it an experience I cherished.

One sunny Monday morning in the summer of 1993, at the age of thirteen, I bumped into my teacher, Maitre J, on my way to my happy place, the maché.

"Miquette, you're such a good student, so smart," he said as I walked. "But I'm sad to tell you that you didn't do well on your trimester final exam."

His words shook me. The trimester final exam was everything—it determined whether a student would pass or have to repeat a grade. Already older than most of my classmates, I was terrified of repeating a grade. At the end of each year, my greatest fear was failing and being held back. I prided myself on being a good student, usually among the top three in my class. My friends and I had prepared so thoroughly for that exam, excited to move up to fifth grade. Yet, something about his timing struck me as odd. Report card day wasn't for another four weeks—why was he telling me now? "If you want to see your exam," he offered, "I can show it to you now. Maybe we can figure out what went wrong."

I was grateful, even moved, that he cared enough to help me understand my mistakes. Eager for answers and not realizing the danger in our world, I followed him back to the school building, which was housed in a church. Inside, classrooms filled each corner, and two makeshift rooms in the back served as classrooms for fifth and sixth grades. As we moved toward the secluded area, he started complimenting me, calling me pretty. Then, in a horrifying instant, he tried to pin me against the wall. He proceeded to touch me in places that made me feel very uncomfortable, and I realized his deceit. He had lured me in with the intention of assaulting me.

In that moment, I felt a surge of terror but also unexpected strength out of my less-than-100-pound body frame. I kicked him as hard as I could and ran.

Outside, I was dazed, almost as if I were watching it all from somewhere else. I couldn't understand why he would try to hurt me—I was only thirteen. *Who could I tell? Would they believe me? Would they blame me for following him?* The questions and doubts flooded my mind, paralyzing me. Fearing judgment and punishment, I kept silent. I forced myself to continue to the maché, buy the items I needed, and return home.

But I was changed. I felt like a part of my dignity had been stripped away, and I carried the weight of it alone. I buried the experience deep inside, hoping to forget. But the memory stayed with me, vivid and unyielding, replaying even decades later.

THE MAJORETTE PROGRAM

In St. Michel, the majorette program was every teenager's dream—a guiding light that shaped us, teaching life skills, discipline, and the value of making good decisions. Open to both boys and girls between the ages of seven and eighteen, it was a vibrant and spirited group that brought the community together. The program was the pride of the town, especially during holidays like Flag Day, when the streets overflowed with people eager to watch the parade.

The performers, dressed in striking white military-style uniforms, marched with precision and grace, their movements synchronized and full of pride. For many, it was more than a performance—it was a symbol of belonging, excellence, and hope. The performance always brought joy and laughter, lifting spirits through rhythm and movement. Every step, spin, and twirl proudly displayed our culture, heritage, and dancing skills. It was a celebration of who we were—and a reminder that even in hard times, beauty and pride could still take center stage.

I dreamed of being one of them—of wearing those shimmering uniforms, hearing the cheers of admiration, and feeling the joy of being part of something meaningful and special.

For years, I stood among the bystanders lining the streets, watching the majorettes entertain the crowd, wishing I could one day be in their place. Eventually, I reached out to a friend in the program who encouraged me to speak to the leader, Mr. Jean. Nervous, I approached him and shared my interest. When he said yes, I was thrilled. But I knew the next step might be harder— convincing my papa to let me join.

At the time, my papa was doing his best to provide for us while my mama worked in Port-au-Prince. I approached him with a hopeful heart, asking for permission to join the majorette program. He was glad I wanted to participate, but he cautioned me gently: I might be able to attend the rehearsals but not the parade itself due to the cost of the uniform. Money was tight, and dreams like this came with a price.

Despite knowing my chances of marching in the parade were slim, I chose to commit to the rehearsals. Three times a week for an entire year, I showed up with the same enthusiasm and hope as the others. Each session fueled my dream of one day taking part in the most anticipated Flag Day Parade on May 18.

As spring approached and excitement filled the air, I tried to push aside the conversation I'd had with my papa. But the reality of our financial situation lingered in the back of my mind. One afternoon after rehearsal, I listened quietly as the other girls talked excitedly about their plans—their uniforms, the joy of performing, and how their neighborhoods were counting down the days to see them march. A wave of sadness washed over me. I couldn't ignore the truth: The uniform was expensive, and despite all my effort, my chances of participating felt heartbreakingly out of reach.

That evening, I gathered my courage and asked my papa if there was any chance I could march in the parade. I could tell his heart longed to say yes, but his pockets told a different story. Yet, after seeing my determination and the effort I'd poured into rehearsals, he made me a promise: He would try to make it happen.

For the next two months, my papa worked diligently, saving every coin he could spare. Finally, the day came when he handed me the 2,000 gourdes I needed to buy the fabric. I held that money in my hands as though it were gold, feeling the heaviness of his sacrifice and the depth of his love. With my head held high and a smile stretching from ear to ear, I walked to the maché to buy the fabric, just as the seamstress had instructed. My excitement bubbled over as I held the fabric in my hands, envisioning the moment it would all come together.

On my way home, I stopped at Saya's home, my majorette mate, to share the good news, beaming with pride. I had no doubt Saya would be part of the parade; her family was financially light years ahead of mine. It didn't even occur to me to ask if she was participating—it just seemed obvious. For someone like her, joining the parade wasn't a question of possibility; it was simply a given.

On May 10, the seamstress informed me that my uniform was ready. One week ahead of the big day. I ran to pick it up. It was perfect. Sharp. Bold. Majestic. I placed it in the armoire at home and checked on it every chance I got, just to admire it. Every night, I practiced my moves in my dreams and in real life. I pictured the parade over and over, hearing the music from the fanfare, seeing the crowd, feeling the joy of every clap and cheer.

Then, just four days before the parade, I went to look at my uniform as I'd done for the past four days—but it was *gone*. I searched every inch of the house—under the armoire, behind the buffet, under the bed, in between every crack. Gone. Panic gripped me. My hands shook. My heart pounded in my chest as tears welled up in my eyes. *No, no, no. This can't be happening.* The thought of telling my papa crushed me. He had worked so hard. I couldn't face him. For two nights, I cried silently, feeling defeated.

But something kept gnawing at me. No one knew where I had placed the uniform—except for Saya. I decided to confront her.

When I arrived at her house, something felt off. Her eyes darted away, and she fidgeted as I asked her directly, "Do you know where my uniform is? I can't find it." She denied it with a shaky voice, but I knew the truth. My heart knew.

This time, I wasn't going to stay silent. I gathered the courage to tell my papa. I expected him to be angry, but instead, he stood beside me. Together, we went to Saya's house. Papa requested to speak with her parents. Calm but firm, he explained how hard he'd worked to buy that fabric and how much this moment meant to me and our family. Saya's parents questioned her, and under her father's stare, she cracked. She admitted it. Minutes later, she returned my uniform.

Through the experiences of that year, I learned so much about my inner strength. Each painful moment—the thief in Gonaïves, my teacher's attempted assault, my missing uniform—revealed something new about the courage growing inside me. I realized that silence was no longer an option, especially when it came to claiming what was mine or standing up for what was right.

But I learned something even deeper: It's okay to speak up for yourself. It's okay to want what belongs to you. That's not pride—it's self-worth. And each time I found my voice, I stepped more fully into the person I was becoming—resilient, brave, and unafraid to take up space in a world that often tried to make me feel small.

On May 18, I stood tall in my crisp white uniform, marching with pride through the streets of St. Michel as people lined the sidewalks to watch the parade. The music swelled, the crowd cheered, and for a moment, I felt unstoppable. I was more than just a girl in a polished uniform—I was living proof that determination, courage, and a voice willing to be heard can turn dreams into reality.

I regret not having pictures from that day. Taking photos required money—something we simply didn't have. Though I have no physical keepsake, the memory is etched deeply in my heart. I can still see that little girl—marching with pride, her steps firm, head held high, and spirit unshaken.

CHAPTER 8
Au Revoir

GROWING UP, MY big sister Keke was my anchor, my confidant, and the one person who understood me better than anyone else. Despite the hardships we endured, she had a way of bringing light into the darkest moments. We were inseparable, sharing not just a makeshift bed in the form of the banana leaves but dreams, secrets, and the unspoken bond that only siblings can have.

Although she was two years older than me, we were in the same grade because she had missed many school months due to unpaid tuition. Falling behind in school only strengthened our bond. We did everything together—homework, chores, and getting ready for school each morning. I can still picture us, side by side, tying our shoes and straightening each other's uniforms and bows, making sure we both looked our best before heading out. It was always the two of us, navigating childhood hand in hand.

We dreamed big together—bold, boundless dreams fueled by the belief that somehow, we would make it. But we didn't just talk about them—we lived them. In our make-believe world, we were unstoppable. We pictured the homes we'd live in, the clothes we'd wear, and most of all, the meals we'd eat. No more hunger pains at night. Plates stacked high with rice, beans, and meat—not just on special occasions but every day. For a moment, it felt real. It felt possible.

Like any siblings, we fought, too—and our fights were ugly. We knew how to push each other's buttons. One moment, we'd be shouting, faces hot with anger. The next, we'd be laughing like nothing had ever been wrong. That's what sisters do. We hurt, we heal, and we hold on to each other.

Two decades after my parents lost their firstborn, tragedy struck again.

In the summer of 1994, Keke had been battling a fever for a few days. Like always, whenever one of us was sick, my mama moved back to St. Michel to care for us, with no return date to Port-au-Prince. She and my papa did everything they could with what little we had—gathering herbal medicines and preparing them with hope in their hearts. Every whispered prayer, every remedy they tried, was a desperate plea for Keke to pull through once more. My parents watched helplessly as she started slipping away. They could no longer afford to take her to a doctor or a nurse; yet hope has a way of convincing you that maybe, just maybe, things will turn around. She had survived before—we truly believed she would again.

But this time was different.

It was a beautiful and deceptively calm morning—the kind that feels gentle and ordinary, giving no hint of the storm to come. My parents had given me money to go to the maché to buy plantains and other essentials to prepare breakfast. I remember the warmth of the sun on my back and the soft hum of daily life around me as I walked to the maché. Nothing felt out of place. Nothing warned me.

But everything changed the moment I returned. From a distance, I saw them—a crowd gathered around our house. Their faces were tight with sorrow, their hands raised to their heads, a language of grief that needed no words. My heart stopped, then pounded so hard it hurt. I knew. I knew. Before anyone said a word, I knew.

It hit me like a blow. I dropped everything—the plantains, the oil, the spices—right there in the dirt. My legs moved before I could think, my body driven by a desperate, frantic need to reach her. I ran, faster than I ever had, straight toward the house, my voice tearing through the air.

"Kekeeeeee ………! Kekeeeee ………!" I screamed her name over and over, each call louder, more desperate than the last. When I reached the house, my cousin grabbed me, her arms wrapping around me with the force of someone trying to stop a car speeding at 100 miles per hour. I crashed into her, my momentum screeching to a sudden halt. I thrashed wildly, desperate to break free. My whole body fought against her grip as I screamed my Keke's name, each cry sharper than the last. But my cousin wouldn't let go. She held on tight, her strength steady against the storm inside me. I was frantic, flailing like a bird trapped in a cage, but no amount of struggle could undo the truth waiting for me inside. None of us imagined it would come to this.

No amount of shouting could bring her back.

The day we lost her, the world seemed to crumble beneath me. Poverty had robbed us of so much already, but this loss felt unbearable—a wound that no time could heal. Keke's laughter, her resilience, and friendship had been the glue holding me together, and without her, I felt lost.

It was another heartache for my parents, who knew the pain of losing their first child. Losing Wilfrid was devastating, but losing Keke was even harder. When Wilfrid died, it was just my parents who carried the grief. But with Keke's death, they had to comfort us, too. They had to be strong for their children while nursing their own broken hearts. It was grief layered with more grief—a load that seemed impossible to carry.

Keke's illness and funeral drained what little my parents had. The goats, the chickens, and even a plot of land had all been sold to buy medicine and food in hopes of nursing her back to life. After her death, life grew even harder. Hunger became a constant, unwelcome guest in our home. Some days, we ate little. Raw mangoes with salt or sugar water with bread sustained us, even when it felt like the world was closing in around us. Other days, we ate nothing at all. Nights like that felt endless, the ache in our stomachs mirroring the ache in our hearts.

But my parents clung to their pride with fierce determination. "Don't say you're hungry," they'd warn us whenever visitors came by. Hunger, they could endure. But the shame of being seen as helpless? That was a burden too heavy to bear.

Poverty steals more than just food—it steals dignity. It turns silence into a shield and pride into a cage. People in the neighborhood would sometimes look at us with disdain, judging my parents for our struggles. Every warning from our parents to hide our hunger was their way of shielding us from a world that mistakes poverty for failure. But for us, as children, that silence carried the bitter taste of pain brought on by starvation.

I could see the truth etched into my parents' faces—the sadness, the helplessness—as they watched us grow thinner with each passing day. Their eyes carried the gravity of their silent struggle, a burden they bore with quiet dignity despite knowing their best efforts were never enough. It was heartbreaking to witness their pain, to feel their sorrow as they desperately tried to shield us from the full weight of our suffering, even as it consumed us all.

FROM MANGO TREES TO CITY STREETS

In the summer of 1995, just one year after losing Keke, my mother delivered life-changing news. "You and Isaac are leaving St. Michel to come live with me and your siblings in Port-au-Prince permanently."

Permanently???

That word hit differently. This wasn't just a visit. This was a *move*.

My little brother Isaac and I exchanged wide-eyed glances, our faces bursting with excitement. Port-au-Prince? The big city? With buildings taller than trees and streets that never slept? We were going to be city kids. No more sweeping dirt yards or hunting for dry firewood in the rain. This was the start of something big.

The next day, I told my best friends, "I'm moving to the city at the end of the summer!" I announced it with pride, as if I'd just been elected president. It was the kind of announcement you don't drop casually—you savor it; you let it hang in the air.

The reactions were mixed. There was excitement, of course— "Port-au-Prince! You're so lucky!"—but also sadness. The kind of sadness that only comes when you know you'll be missing your partner in crime. But beneath it all, I also sensed some jealousy. The kind of jealousy that sits in the corner of a smile and says, "Why not me?" They hid it well, but I could feel it. I understood. If it were one of them moving, I'd probably feel the same way.

The night before we left, sleep barely found me. I lay in bed, eyes wide open, heart pounding like it was New Year's Eve. The thrill of going to Port-au-Prince was unlike anything else—more than just a trip, it was a step into another world.

Excitement kept me restless, but more than that, I was determined not to miss the pickup truck. The driver made his rounds at 4 a.m., announcing his arrival with a single, deafening blast of his horn—no knocking, no calling, just one long, soul-rattling HOOOOOONK. It was his way of saying, "I'm here. Get in or get left." If you missed it, that was your problem—I wasn't about to let that happen.

Upon hearing the hooooonk, I shot up like a rocket, adrenaline surging through me. This was it. My papa was already up, waiting with my bag—and by that, I mean, a 25-pound rice sack repurposed for travel. No suitcase. No backpack. Just the same kind of bag we stored beans in. My "luggage" had all the sophistication of a potato sack, but I didn't care. Bigger things were ahead—like becoming a city girl.

Papa carefully tied up the bag, making sure my few personal items were secure. He also loaded up some produce and charcoal for my mom because in Haiti, no trip is complete without sending "a little something." If a family member is traveling, you send plantains, coffee, avocados, or charcoal with them.

As we loaded onto the truck, I looked back at Papa. He hugged me tight, the kind of hug that feels like it's supposed to last a whole year. His eyes were proud but sad. "*Bon chans*," he said softly. "Good luck." Those two words carried so much. He didn't give me a grand speech, but he didn't have to. I knew he was counting on me to do something with this opportunity.

The truck rattled and jerked as we pulled away from the only home I had ever known. I sat on a wooden bench with Isaac by my side, our legs dangling off the edge. The wind whipped through my hair, and the cool morning air hit my face. I waved, shouting my goodbyes like I was royalty on a farewell tour.

As the truck rumbled through my family's neighborhood, every twist and turn of the path felt familiar—paths I had walked a thousand times before. But this time, I wasn't walking. I wasn't coming back later that afternoon. This was goodbye.

With each bump of the road, I turned my head to catch one last glimpse of everything I loved. My heart tugged with every sight that passed.

"Goodbye, Guerlande's house," I whispered, thinking of all the afternoons we spent playing hopscotch until our feet were covered in dust.

"Goodbye, Juno's house," I said with a small smile, remembering the boy I had a crush on—the one who liked me back but was too afraid of my dad to ever say it out loud.

"Goodbye, Anouse's house," I whispered, my heart heavy with memories of her warm smile. I could still see her face lit up with joy as she shared her sugar cane with me. We bonded over our love for flowers, spending countless hours exchanging plants to brighten each other's homes. Those moments were simple but full of love—the kind of love that stays with you long after you've said goodbye.

"Goodbye, Michou's house," I said softly, my eyes lingering on the kenepe tree that had given us so many sweet summer memories. I could almost taste the tangy fruit on my tongue, recalling the laughter and sticky fingers shared beneath its shade. That tree was a part of our story, a place where joy bloomed as freely as the fruit it bore. I knew I would miss it deeply.

Then, my eyes landed on the mango trees. Tall, wide, and generous in every season. "Goodbye, mango trees," I said, this time with a little more emotion. These trees had been better to me than some people. They had fed me when there was no food at home, given me shade when the sun blazed too hot, and offered a place to rest when I needed to be still. These trees had never judged me. They just gave. It felt wrong not to thank them.

The well came next. That well. I had fought so many battles there—not just for water but for my pride. I had fought with girls who thought they could skip the line, fought for space to fill my bucket, and fought my own patience on days when the line never seemed to move. I thought about every argument, every time someone splashed me with water on purpose, and every triumphant moment when I finally filled my bucket to the brim. "Goodbye, well," I said with a sigh. "You didn't make it easy, but you made me stronger."

With each farewell, my chest tightened. It wasn't just places I was leaving behind—it was pieces of me. My friends, the trees, the well—all of them had shaped me in some way. I wasn't sure what would fill their place in Port-au-Prince. *Would I have mango trees there? Would I have friends to argue with and laugh with like I had with Anouse, Guerlande, and Edline? Would I have a place where I could just be?*

The truck rattled on, and I sat on the edge, my hands gripping the wooden frame as the wind whipped around me. Each turn of the road felt like another thread of childhood being pulled away. I didn't know it then, but I was already starting to learn something about life—that every goodbye hurts a little because it's also a reminder of how much you loved what you had even when it was not always easy.

I squeezed my eyes shut for a moment, letting the warm breeze wash over my face. The familiar scent of the earth rose around me, etching itself into my memory. A lump formed in my throat as I thought of my dear sister Keke—gone far too soon. She would not be coming on this journey with me. I whispered one last time, "Au revoir, St. Michel." My voice trembled. *I will never forget you—not the laughter of my friends, not the rustle of the mango trees, and certainly not the place that made me who I am.*

CHAPTER 9

Not What It Seems

I WAS SO excited to finally live in the house my mama had built in the big city. But my excitement faded quickly when I saw just how small it was—a single-room structure with a tin roof that barely kept out the scorching sun. It was no bigger than a backyard shed, yet eight of us lived within its cramped walls.

Inside, there were only two twin beds and a tiny dining table. At night, the beds were claimed by my older siblings—two per bed—while the younger ones, including me, slept on the floor. My space was under the dining table, a small corner where I curled up at night, trying to find comfort on the hard floor.

Shortly after arriving, I entered sixth grade. My mama, busy with work, tasked my siblings with finding a public school for me. But in Haiti, even public education—meant for low-income families—was out of reach without the right connections. For the poor, securing a spot was nearly impossible.

After exhausting all options, my mama, heartbroken by the cost of education in Port-au-Prince, enrolled me in a private school. Over 90 percent of schools in Haiti are private, and even the most affordable ones were a financial burden. To save money, I was placed in the afternoon session, which cost less than the morning sessions.

I knew the depth of that sacrifice, and I was determined to make the most of it. My dream of becoming a nurse had deepened when Keke became sick. I watched how the nurses had cared for her—with compassion, tenderness, and a calm resolve that left a lasting impression on me. Their presence was a source of comfort in a time of fear. They couldn't cure her, but they treated her with dignity. That experience etched something permanent into my heart: I wanted to be like them. I wanted to serve and to bring peace where there was pain.

My brother Pidens, though six years older than me, was in the same grade due to financial struggles that had repeatedly delayed his schooling. Attending the same school as him gave me a sense of security, but it was also a painful reminder of how poverty dictated the pace of our lives, holding us back in ways we couldn't control.

My favorite subjects at school were biology, social studies, and French literature, and after passing my *certificat* exam—a standardized test required before entering middle school—I transferred to Collège Mixte de L'Espérance in Delmas 65. This time, I was enrolled in the morning session, which felt like a privilege. Morning classes were more challenging, more prestigious, and of course, more expensive.

Every day, I walked an hour to school, often on an empty stomach, with no money for a *tap-tap* ride—the colorful, box-style trucks used as taxis in Haiti. Unlike St. Michel, where I could always find something to eat from the land, Port-au-Prince offered no such solace. There were no mango trees within reach, no sugar cane fields to quiet my hunger. I relied on the kindness of friends, hoping someone would share a snack with me.

The rainy season was the worst. Even a light rain turned our home into a leaking mess. We stayed up late, placing cups and buckets to catch the water pouring from the ceiling, while plastic sheets covered everything in a desperate attempt to keep our few belongings dry. It was tedious, miserable, and exhausting. By morning, we were too tired to function, our bodies aching from the restless night.

At school, exhaustion weighed on me like a heavy blanket. My eyelids drooped, my mind struggled to focus, and inevitably, I would doze off in class. My teachers grew irritated, scolding me for not paying attention. They couldn't understand why I was always so tired during the rainy season—and, of course, I was too embarrassed to tell them the truth. How could I explain that sleep was impossible when I spent the night catching rainwater, while other children lay peacefully in their beds? Instead, I stayed silent, carrying the exhaustion and shame, knowing that poverty had stolen yet another piece of my childhood.

But the shame didn't end at school. My heart sank whenever my friends eagerly invited me to their homes, where the contrast between their lives and mine was painfully stark. Their houses had sturdy roofs, separate rooms, and real beds—things I only dreamed of. Whenever they asked to visit my house, I always had an excuse ready. No matter what time they suggested, I suddenly had something "already planned." I wasn't just avoiding them—I was protecting myself from the humiliation of exposing my reality.

Pidens and I had even rehearsed scenarios in case a friend unexpectedly insisted on coming over. We always had a reason—our parents weren't home, we had errands to run, we had to visit a relative. Anything to keep them from seeing the truth. Only my absolute best friend, Bea—whom I met at school and instantly bonded with—had ever seen where I lived. No one else. That small house, a reflection of our struggles, felt too vulnerable to expose.

Poverty didn't just dictate where we lived—it affected our pride. It affected *everything*. Even something as simple as going to school became a battle against a system that seemed designed to keep people like us from moving forward, a shared experience in the developing world.

School fees remained a constant struggle. The humiliation of being sent home during exam time because we couldn't pay was something I relived over and over again. My mama worked without rest, but it was never enough.

Her job was grueling—she cared for severely disabled residents in a group home, their ages ranging from three to fifty. Many had severe and extreme physical deformities and limited mobility, and without mechanical lifts, moving them required immense physical strength and stamina. The job was so exhausting that staff often took unpaid days off, unable to push through. Seeing an opportunity, I decided I would take on their shifts.

But I knew convincing my mama wouldn't be easy. She had fought to give me a chance at education, to keep me from the same hardships she endured. Asking her to let me work was asking her to watch me step into a struggle she had desperately tried to shield me from.

So, I presented my case the only way I knew how—through the reality we both faced.

"Mom," I said, "I know you do everything you can to pay my tuition, but it's not enough. I'm tired of the humiliation of being kicked out of class, of students making fun of me when I have to leave because of missed payments. Let me help. I promise it's not a permanent solution, but I can't finish school if we can't pay for it."

Her eyes filled with sadness. I could see the weight she carried—the long, backbreaking hours she worked just to give us a better future. She didn't want me to know that kind of struggle. She didn't want me to live her life.

Her hesitation was palpable, her silence heavy. But eventually, with a deep breath, she nodded.

For two years I juggled working from 6 a.m. to 2 p.m., then heading straight to school from 3 to 8 p.m. Every shift I worked felt like a quiet victory. Each paycheck was proof that I could lighten my mama's load, even if just a little. Every hour spent working was a step closer to staying in school, to holding on to the dream we had fought so hard to protect.

Poverty tried to take everything from me—my childhood, my education, my future—but I refused to let it win.

BEYOND THE BOUGAINVILLEA

In the summer of 1998, an opportunity I never expected came my way.

Mommy Carme, the woman who asked me about my birthday, was an affluent woman in Port-au-Prince and a good friend of my mama. Although their social class and socioeconomic status were worlds apart, she never let that define how she treated others. Her kindness was like a breeze on a hot day. She lived in a beautiful home with a large yard full of trees and flowers. I loved going to her house to help—every time I stepped through her gate, it felt like entering a different world. Her home gave me space to dream, to imagine a life beyond poverty. She treated me with warmth and dignity, always looking out for my well-being. Mommy Carme wasn't just my mama's friend—she was a quiet light in my life.

One day, Mommy Carme introduced me to a friend, who needed a nanny for the summer to care for her three nieces visiting from the United States. The offer was simple but life-changing: 3,000 gourdes a month—about $30 at the time.

When I heard the amount, my heart nearly burst with excitement. *Three thousand gourdes?!* It was more than my mama was making. For the first time, I felt the thrill of financial independence. With that income, I could finally save enough to pay for an entire year of school fees. No more sitting at home while other students walked past me on their way to class. No more humiliation from being sent home for unpaid tuition.

The job required me to live with the children six days a week. Their home was located in a more affluent part of the city, where public transportation was scarce—most residents had private cars. As a result, I had to walk nearly an hour and a half just to reach the main road where I could catch a tap-tap home. Saturdays were my only day off—the only window I had to see my family. I'd leave in the afternoon and return on Sundays, just in time to start the week all over again.

It wouldn't be easy, but I didn't care. I had a purpose now. I felt like I held the power to change my future.

At around 4:30 p.m., I was picked up by my boss and taken to my new home for the summer. I could barely contain my excitement. My heart raced with anticipation; each beat filled with wonder. *What would the house look like? Would it be like the ones I'd seen in magazines?* I imagined my room—surely, it would be nice, unlike anything I'd ever had before.

As we drove through the neighborhood, my eyes darted from window to window, trying to take in every detail. The streets were lined with towering walls draped in bright pink bougainvillea blooms, their colors so vivid they didn't seem real. The air smelled different, too—cleaner, softer, carrying the quiet promise of something better. Every turn, every glimpse, made my heart swell with hope.

Then we arrived …

My boss' house was more than a house—it was a fortress of beauty and wealth. High concrete walls wrapped around it like a secret no one was meant to see. Lush gardens surrounded the house, with palm trees swaying and colorful flowers everywhere. The house itself was grand, its whitewashed walls almost glowing in the golden light of the evening. For a girl who had grown up sweeping dirt floors, this felt like stepping into another world.

But beauty has layers, and I would soon see the cracks beneath it.

The reality inside those walls was nothing like I had imagined. While the grand house boasted over 5,000 square feet and multiple empty bedrooms, workers were crammed into tiny box-like rooms at the back of the house. Comfort wasn't a consideration. I was assigned a narrow space to share with the cook—just enough room for two foam mattresses. My excitement dimmed, but I reminded myself why I was there: to pay for school and fight for a future I refused to give up on.

The contrast between "family" and "help" was stark and undeniable. Workers entered the main house solely to clean—never to rest. Sitting on one of the family's plush sofas was a punishable offense, as I witnessed firsthand. Grown men and women were humiliated, sometimes even fired, for the simple act of sitting on the pristine furniture. The message was clear: They served the house but were never truly welcome in it.

The separation extended to everything, even our plates and utensils. The family ate from smooth porcelain dishes fit for magazine spreads, while we ate from thin, flimsy plastic plates that could blow away with a gust of wind. I often stared at the difference, wondering if food tasted better on porcelain. *Did rice feel softer? Did beans taste richer?*

One day, that line between "family" and "help" was drawn even sharper. I had put the baby I was watching down for a nap and rushed to the kitchen to fill my water bottle. But when I heard her cry, I quickly set the bottle on the kitchen counter and ran back to soothe her. Moments later, my boss stormed in. Her eyes darted around the kitchen like she was searching for something filthy.

"WHOSE WATER BOTTLE IS THIS?" she snapped, her voice cold and cutting.

My heart dropped. I knew it was mine, but fear gripped me. She lifted it with the tips of her fingers, holding it away from her body like it was contaminated. The unspoken message was clear: You don't belong here.

"Is this yours?" she asked, eyes locked on me.

"Oui, Madame," I said softly, my eyes on the floor.

Her voice went cold. "What if my kids or nieces drank from it, not knowing it was yours?"

Those words cut me deeper than I can explain. Her tone, the look of disgust, the way she acted like I was a threat. It wasn't just about the water bottle. It was about me. It was about what I was in her eyes—a poor girl who could bring harm to her children with a sip of water. It was the first time I realized that poverty, in their world, wasn't just a condition. It was a contagion. Something to be feared. Something to be kept away.

That moment changed me. I decided, right then and there, that I would do whatever it took to rise above this life. I will stay in school. I will not be the girl with the plastic plate. I will not be the girl whose water bottle brings disgust. No matter how hard the journey, I vowed to carve a path to a life where I would never feel that way again.

I worked hard that summer. I poured love into those three children, even when their aunt didn't see my worth. I showed up every day with purpose. I finished the summer with enough money to pay for an entire year of school fees. When I handed the money to my mother, she hugged me so tightly I thought my ribs would crack.

I never told Mommy Carme about some of what I experienced that summer—she would have been too upset about it. I simply chose instead to be grateful for the income that it provided me. But that time left scars—invisible ones.

CHAPTER 10

A Spark of Hope

THE SPRING OF 1999 marked a decade since my parents made the most agonizing decision of their lives—a decision no parent should ever have to face. Ten years earlier, out of love and desperation, they had placed my sister, Farah, and niece, Cherline (whom I refer to as my sister), in an orphanage, where they were quickly adopted by a family in the United States.

The cost of that decision weighed heavily on our family every single day since. The void left by Farah and Cherline was filled with unanswered questions and lingering heartache. *Were they thriving? Were they safe? Did they feel loved—or abandoned?* My parents' minds were haunted by the unknown, their hearts scarred by the unbearable mix of love, loss, and the painful reality of trying to protect their family.

Then, in May of that year, something miraculous happened.

Word reached us that my sisters' adoptive father was coming to Haiti to meet us—*us.* For years, Farah and Cherline had belonged to an unknown family, living a life I could only imagine. Over the years, we had received a couple of sporadic letters from these unknown parents—John and Mary Lee—but it was never often, and it was never enough for our hearts to feel fully content.

When my mama shared the news with us, I froze. John? Coming to Haiti? To meet us?! My heart pounded with excitement and fear, a flood of emotions swirling inside me. For years, I had wondered what kind of family the girls were part of. *Did they love them the way we did? Did they hold them, protect them, and cherish them the way we had?* These questions were even more important knowing the heart-wrenching rumors that were circulating about adopted children in St. Michel.

The day of the meeting, I was nervous. I kept flattening my dress and smoothing my hair, hoping to look presentable. My heart was pounding so loudly, I was sure my mama could hear it. I practiced the limited conversational English I had learned in school in preparation for the meeting. I didn't know what to expect, but I knew I had to be brave.

I'm not exactly sure why my mama chose me to meet him first, but I was thrilled to be the one. Maybe it was because I spoke a little bit of English and could introduce myself without an interpreter—sometimes I joke that it was because I'm her favorite child. Whatever the reason, I was proud and eager. Of course, everyone else would have their chance to meet John eventually.

When my mama and I arrived at the guesthouse John was staying at, we knocked on the gate, and John came to open it. He wasn't at all what I had imagined. I had expected someone serious, maybe even intimidating or distant. But instead, he was warm, kind, and gentle. He smiled as he approached, his eyes scanning us with quiet curiosity, as if searching for something familiar.

I stood frozen for a moment, nerves holding me in place. But I took a deep breath, clenched my hands, and stepped forward. "Hi, I'm from Miquette, and this is my mama, Rose." Nerves got the best of me, I even forgot how to introduce my own name.

John smiled, his eyes crinkling at the corners. He reached out his hand, and in that small gesture, something shifted inside me. I didn't feel like "the poor village girl." I felt seen. I felt like Miquette.

We sat together, and for the first time, we talked about Farah and Cherline—not as memories but as real people. John told us about their new lives, how they were happy, healthy, and doing well in school. My heart swelled with relief. For ten years, I had wondered if they were okay. Finally, I knew.

John shared stories that made them feel real again. Cherline loved reading and soccer. Farah had a passion for sports, especially track and field. Both of them were active in John's church. It felt like I was getting them back, piece by piece.

John also shared a bit about his family. They lived in a small town called Detroit Lakes in Minnesota. He and his wife, Mary, had two biological sons, Dan and Carl. He was a pastor of three Lutheran church parishes, and Mary was a registered nurse. Hearing that Mary was a nurse sparked something in me. I had dreamed of becoming a nurse, too. Knowing that my sisters were being raised by a nurse and a pastor gave me comfort. It made me feel like they were safe, like they were in the care of people who understood the importance of nurturing and healing.

There was so much I wanted to ask John. Questions about my sisters, about his family, about their lives in an unfamiliar world. But with my limited English, I had to keep it short. Each question had to be carefully chosen, like picking fruit from a tree where you're only allowed to take one or two.

When my English ran out, I was especially grateful for the French woman who interpreted for us. She had come to Haiti to pick up her daughter, whom she had been waiting to adopt for years, and it was arranged that she would translate for John while she was there.

Her presence gave me the courage to ask questions I might've been too shy or uncertain to voice on my own. She was my bridge to understanding, and I clung to every word she translated as if each one brought me closer to the family I longed to know.

At one point, I couldn't hold back the most important questions any longer. "Do they know us?" I asked. "Do they know who we are?"

John leaned forward, his face serious but kind. "Yes," he said softly. "They know. We've told them about you."

Tears blurred my vision. *They know us. They hadn't forgotten us. Even in another country, with another family, they still carried us with them.*

"Do they remember *me*?" I asked, my voice barely a whisper. "Do they remember that I was their sister?"

John nodded. "Yes, Miquette. They know you were their big sister. They know how much you loved them."

Those words broke something open inside me. Every emotion I had buried for ten years came rushing back—joy, pain, relief, and grief all at once. I had spent so long wondering if they remembered me—if the days I spent carrying them, feeding them, playing with them—had been forgotten. But they knew. They still remembered. They remembered us. And my mama, standing beside me, was filled with joy upon hearing such a beautiful affirmation. It was as if a missing piece of our story had finally returned.

Later I learned that John and Mary had tried their best to keep us connected with the girls, consistently sending letters and cards, but for reasons beyond our control, only a few made it through to us, despite their efforts. Just before his arrival, we actually received a few of the letters they had sent *years* earlier. Within their letters, they always tried to make sure my mama knew the girls were safe and healthy.

But meeting John in person brought all of that to life. His actions, his words, his gentle presence—it confirmed what I had only heard about or imagined from afar.

For the rest of the week, I visited John at his guesthouse every day. Sometimes my other siblings would join me, but I was the one who showed up consistently—day after day. Something in me needed to be there, to soak up every moment, every word, every connection. I didn't want to miss a single chance to bridge the gap between our worlds. He welcomed me for dinner every night. He asked me about my childhood in St. Michel, where we lived without running water or electricity. I shared my love for school and the heartbreak of being sent home when we couldn't pay the fees. John listened with compassion, asking thoughtful questions about my education, my dreams, and my future.

He taught me songs like "Jesus Loves the Little Children" and "God Will Make a Way," and helped me practice English. We sang the "Johnny Appleseed" prayer before meals. Sitting at a table, sharing food and conversation, felt magical. It was a glimpse of a world where education was possible, and aspirations weren't crushed by poverty.

During John's time in Haiti, he spoke with several people—including Mommy Carme. She spoke English, which allowed her to advocate for us and share our family's story in a way we couldn't. She told John about my parents' constant struggle to keep us in school, and I believe her words stirred something in his heart.

After speaking with Mommy Carme, John reached out to Gladys to express his desire to help me come to the US. It was Gladys who had placed my sisters with the Lee family, so it made sense that John would seek her guidance about bringing me to the US, too.

Having witnessed unfulfilled promises before, Gladys was no stranger to the heartbreak caused by empty words. She had seen the disappointment that followed when well-meaning people failed to follow through. With firm resolve, she told John, "Please do not break a poor Haitian girl's heart." Her words were a plea for honesty and accountability.

On our last day together, John asked me, through an interpreter, "Miquette, if I convince a Rotary Club in the United States to sponsor you, would you be interested in coming to the US to study for one year?" His words hung in the air, almost too big to believe—an opportunity that felt both unreal and life-changing.

In that moment, time seemed to stand still.

I froze. *Did I hear that right?* My chest tightened with emotion. I didn't answer with words—I just ran up and hugged him. The interpreter laughed, "Do I need to translate that answer?"

John chuckled, "I think I got it."

There were no guarantees, but I felt hope—real hope. The dream that had always lingered, dim but never extinguished—the dream of becoming a nurse—suddenly felt possible again.

When my family heard there was a chance I could go to the US, they shared in my joy. My siblings pooled their savings so I could take private English lessons. They understood what this opportunity could mean for all of us. In Haiti, having just one family member in the US can change everything.

When it was time for John to leave, it felt like I was losing something precious all over again. But this time, it was different. I knew where my sisters were. I knew who was caring for them. And I knew they hadn't forgotten me.

Before he left, John turned to us and said, "I will always take care of them. You don't have to worry."

My mama reached for his hand, tears welling in her eyes. "Mèsi" she whispered, her voice cracking with relief. For so long, she had carried the heavy burden of guilt—feeling like a failure, a bad mother, as though she was no longer needed by her daughters. But John's words lifted that burden, replacing it with hope. Hope not only for her daughters' future but also for the possibility of reuniting with them one day.

Meeting John in person transformed everything. His presence made all the difference. The moment he looked at my mother and said, "You don't have to worry," something shifted. The heart-wrenching decision she had made so many years before suddenly felt not only bearable—but right.

We said our goodbyes at the guesthouse on his last night. I tried to memorize every detail of him—his face, his voice, his kindness. I wanted to lock it all in my heart, knowing I might never see him again. Although he had offered to help me come to the US, there was no guarantee it would happen. Still, he wasn't just a visitor; he was the man who had given me my sisters back.

That night, back at my house, I curled up on the floor mat, replaying John's words over and over: "They know you were their big sister. They know how much you loved them." I whispered it to myself like a lullaby, letting the words wash over me. For the first time in ten years, I fell asleep with peace in my heart.

My sisters weren't gone. They were just living a different story. And somehow, in the middle of it, we had found each other again.

I didn't know it then, but meeting John wasn't the end of the story.

PART TWO

Big Dreams

CHAPTER 11
Moving Mountains

IN JUNE 2000, Deanna, a member of the Detroit Lakes Noon Rotary Club in Minnesota, sat at the club's annual Changing of the Guard Dinner—an evening where members and guests gathered to celebrate, reflect, and pass the baton to the incoming president.

As the event wound down, Deanna was standing in the lobby when John Lee, who was there as a guest, approached her with a bold and unexpected request. He wanted to bring a poor girl from Haiti to the United States as an exchange student and asked if Deanna's club would sponsor her.

For those who aren't familiar with Rotary Club, it's a global humanitarian organization with over 1.4 million members in more than 200 countries. Its members—known as Rotarians—are professionals, leaders, and volunteers united by a common motto: "Service Above Self." They seek to create lasting change in communities both locally and globally by working to promote peace, improve health, support education, strengthen economies, and protect the environment.

One of the many opportunities Rotary offers is the Youth Exchange Program, which is for students entering their junior year of high school. The goal is to create global citizens and build skills for peace and conflict resolution. They believe that a well-rounded teen is more likely to be a well-rounded citizen. For students entering the Rotary Youth Exchange Program, the process is clear: Candidates are selected at least a year in advance, and host clubs must meet strict criteria to be approved.

Deanna explained the challenges to John. Their club already had a student arriving in August, with host families in place. Additionally, there was a requirement that host students live with Rotarians, which posed another hurdle, as John and Mary were not members of Rotary.

But John was insistent, so Deanna encouraged him to join Rotary to help meet the requirements. John readily agreed, noting that his father had been a dedicated Rotarian for many years and that he deeply admired Rotary's work. Joining would be an honor for him. This decision added momentum to an already unlikely process.

Deanna, inspired by John's determination, promised to make some calls. True to her word, the very next day she reached out to the district governor at the time, Jack. He was no stranger to Haiti—he had worked on numerous projects there throughout the 1990s and was deeply familiar with both the challenges and the potential of the country.

With his profound understanding of the country's struggles—the relentless poverty, the overwhelming barriers to opportunity, and the resilience of its people—Jack didn't hesitate to offer his help. His willingness to step in marked the beginning of a miraculous collaborative effort rooted in compassion.

Jack quickly mobilized support, reaching out to influential figures, including Dr. Guy Theodore, a Haitian Rotarian and assistant district governor in Haiti, as well as the district coordinator for exchange students. Recognizing the complexity of the situation, he even engaged Rotary International headquarters in Evanston, Illinois. This was no ordinary case. It required the attention and intervention of senior Rotary leaders.

After a thorough review, the process was approved. While Rotary International couldn't directly grant a visa, which I would need to study in the US for the year, their involvement proved instrumental in making it a possibility. Their collective efforts lent credibility and support.

In the summer of 2000, through Gladys' office, I received the electrifying news: the Rotary Club in Detroit Lakes, Minnesota, had accepted my application as a youth exchange student. My acceptance wasn't just a surprise; it was truly a testament to the miraculous power of God. He was weaving a tapestry of miracles for me and my family. Mountains had to be moved for this to work. The normal process had been overturned, defying logic and normalcy, so I could walk through a door of great opportunity. When God is at work, nothing is impossible!

At the time, I had no idea all of this was unfolding on my behalf—the numerous phone calls and conversations with various leaders. I wouldn't learn the full story until much later.

My dream of becoming a high school graduate and studying nursing felt even more within reach. However, this was just one major step in the journey. The next challenge lay in Haiti. The Detroit Lakes Noon Rotary Club could not act alone. The organization works in partnership with local host clubs, and the collaboration between the clubs in the US and Haiti presented its own unique hurdles.

With limited resources, I was unsure where to start. Thankfully, John had already spoken with Gladys, who introduced me to Dr. Claude Surena, a respected pediatrician and member of the Pétion-Ville Rotary Club.

Meeting Dr. Surena was intimidating. I was accustomed to speaking only with those from backgrounds similar to mine. I was not sure what to expect. But Dr. Surena was polite and kind, explaining how the Rotary Club's Youth Exchange Program worked and inviting me to their weekly meeting, where he introduced me as a club candidate.

The day of the meeting, I donned my best outfit, carefully carrying my nice shoes in a bag to avoid getting them dusty and set out for the Pétion-Ville Country Club. The journey was eye-opening. I walked through a neighborhood of grand houses, lined with trees and bougainvillea-covered walls. Before entering the compound of the club, I dusted off my feet, slipped into my good shoes, and took a deep breath.

As I stepped inside, I was awestruck by the beauty around me—marble-like tiles gleaming under the lights, elegant furnishings perfectly arranged, and attendees dressed in their finest. It was, without a doubt, the most luxurious place I had ever seen.

Dr. Surena greeted me at the entrance with a reassuring smile, instantly easing my nerves. He guided me through the room, introducing me to several of the members in attendance. When it was time to dine, he led me to the buffet, where an incredible spread of food awaited. For the first time in my life, I experienced a five-course meal. The variety of options was overwhelming, and I felt like royalty as servers moved gracefully through the room, offering various drinks to choose from.

After dinner, Dr. Surena stood before the room and introduced me to the club as their candidate for the Youth Exchange Program. I didn't fully understand the magnitude of what it all meant, but I knew one thing for certain—it was a chance to go to the US and hopefully, change my family's future.

When the meeting ended, members made their way to their cars and drove off. Not wanting them to see me walking, I waited until they had all left. Then, I quietly made my way to the main road to catch a tap-tap home.

That night, I returned home to my family, who eagerly awaited every detail. My brothers asked about the food, my sister wanted to know if I met anyone famous, and my parents wondered if the club had agreed to sponsor me. The excitement in the room was palpable, like a family who'd received the best news of their lives. For all of us, the possibility of me studying in the United States held so much promise.

Paperwork soon began arriving from the Noon Rotary Club in Detroit Lakes, and since I had no way to receive mail directly, it was sent to Gladys. Every time I went to her office to pick up a document, I was filled with joy and excitement, knowing that each piece of paper brought me closer to realizing my dream.

It was my moment, my once-in-a-lifetime opportunity, and I was ready to tackle it with everything I had.

As part of the program, students were required to complete a doctor and a dental visit before departing for their host country. At nineteen, I had never been to a dentist—not for lack of need, but because it simply wasn't an option. Toothaches and abscesses were common due to poor nutrition, but there was no money for dental care. When we saw that a dental record was required, my family huddled up to make a plan. Although no one had funds to spare, my sister Sandra emptied her small savings account, realizing there was no other way. The dentist found extensive issues, with multiple cavities requiring fillings, and Sandra's selfless sacrifice meant I could get it done.

I also needed lab work and a physical exam. This, too, was financially challenging, but my family didn't want to risk missing any requirement that might hinder my visa application. They sacrificed food and other basic needs to make sure I could complete the necessary medical care and paperwork.

Another requirement was photos of my home, a pet, my best friend, and my hobbies. Ironically, this was the hardest part for me. I had always been ashamed of our one-room home, an eyesore that I never allowed friends to see. I didn't have a pet, and while I loved singing, reading was a hobby I only dreamed of, as I had no access to books.

Despite these challenges, we completed everything as best we could. We sent the documents to the Noon Rotary Club and anxiously awaited the next step.

FLIGHT RISK

In August 2000, I had an appointment with the US consul general in Haiti to determine whether I would be granted a visa to study in the US for the year. John decided to make a quick trip to Haiti to personally bring me to the US afterward. He was certain I would be granted the visa and had even purchased my plane ticket, but he knew I would need help navigating the airport and customs, so he'd come himself to ensure everything went smoothly.

The trip was a major sacrifice for the Lee family, as it happened to be around the same time they had planned to drop off their second son, Carl, at college in Duluth, Minnesota, for the first semester of his freshman year. Mary was heartbroken at the thought of doing it alone; saying goodbye to your child at college is never easy, and the emotional toll of that day felt heavy.

But John, determined, looked at her and said, "I'm sorry, Mary, you have to do this alone. I have to go to Haiti. Miquette won't get out without me." His words were prophetic. His presence in Haiti would mean the difference between stepping onto that plane or being turned back.

With that decision, John left Detroit Lakes on August 27, stayed overnight with his good friends Tom and Sue, and left his car with them in Minneapolis. The next morning, he flew to West Palm Beach, Florida, stayed overnight again, and then boarded a plane to Haiti, carrying with him not just his own hope but mine, my family's, and everyone who believed in the power of dreams.

A missionary couple named Karl and Anne picked John up at the airport. Karl served as the pastor of an English-speaking church in Haiti called Quisqueya Chapel, and together, he and his wife also managed the guesthouse where John would be staying. It was the same guesthouse he had stayed in a year earlier, though at that time, Karl and Anne were not yet the managers. Having them there this time was a true delight—they were among the kindest and most caring people I had ever met.

I waited anxiously for John's arrival at the guesthouse, unaware of how much his presence would change everything.

When I saw John, an indescribable surge of strength and confidence washed over me. He was like a grounding force, a reminder that I wasn't in this endeavor alone. For so long, the idea of leaving Haiti had felt like a distant dream, but with John here beside me, that dream felt tangible and within reach.

On August 29, the night before my visa appointment, I felt a whirlwind of emotions stirring within me. I carefully ironed one of the only two nice dresses I owned, a dress John had helped me buy during his previous visit, and placed my black shoes in the corner, ready to wear for the big day. My family held a long prayer session, each of them taking turns laying hands on me, pleading with God to grant me favor. They prayed that the US consul general would see how much this opportunity meant to us and approve my visa.

After the prayer, I lay down in my usual sleeping spot on the hard floor, but sleep was elusive. I was too wired, my mind racing with endless "what ifs." I kept imagining the blue sky, picturing myself high above the clouds, and wondering if, in just a few days, this dream could become my reality.

The next day held the potential to transform not only my life but the life of my entire family. In less than twelve hours, I would face the most important meeting of my life. My encounter with the consul general would determine my future.

That morning, I put on my dress and clutched the yellow envelope containing all my documents, including my passport. I stood in line with about 400 others, all seeking entry to the United States, the land of opportunity. After waiting under the scorching sun for over an hour, I finally stepped inside the consulate for my interview.

When my turn came, the interviewing officer, a man in his forties, greeted me with, "What's up?" I froze. That phrase wasn't in any of my English lessons, and I didn't know how to respond. As I stumbled, he went on to ask why I wanted to go to the US. I did my best to explain the Rotary Youth Exchange Program. But instead of asking more, he stamped my passport, handed back my envelope, and said, "You are not qualified" and stated I was a "flight risk." I had no idea what the term meant, but I knew it wasn't good.

"NEXT!" he called, dismissing me without another word.

My world collapsed. I felt all our sacrifices pressing down on me. *Why, God? We did everything we could—prayed, paid for doctor visits, gathered all the documents—why was this happening?*

Outside, John was waiting in the sun. He saw my downcast face and immediately understood. "Did you get it?" he asked.

With tears in my eyes, I shook my head and whispered, "No."

John's face registered shock. "What? How? You have everything!"

I mumbled, "They said I'm a flight risk."

John didn't understand, and honestly, neither did I.

John immediately wanted to schedule another appointment. However, the normal process requires that an applicant wait for six months before re-applying after being rejected for a visa. Well … that plan was not going to work for John. He was determined to bring me back to the US. He had come to Haiti for that very reason. He had asked his parish to give him just a few days since he thought the trip would take less than one week.

Determined to get answers, John tried to speak with the interviewing officer, but he was dismissed again and again. Eventually, we drove back to the guesthouse, both of us grappling with disappointment. But John, ever persistent, began to think of a Plan B.

After the visa denial, John composed a letter to the US Embassy expressing his disappointment. Before sending it, he contacted his wife, Mary, who was equally heartbroken by the news. Determined not to give up, Mary reached out to her friend Sharon Josephson, who served as the office administrator for Minnesota Congressional Representative Colin Peterson. Sharon invited Mary to her office on September 1, where, together, they called the US Consulate in Haiti, requesting to speak with the consul general.

The receptionist informed them that he was busy and suggested leaving a message. Aware that this could lead to indefinite delays, Sharon insisted on holding. After a prolonged wait, her persistence paid off; the call was transferred to Consul General Roger Daley. Sharon requested an immediate meeting for me to meet him with John present. That afternoon, John received a call informing him of a new appointment on September 5 at the consulate with the consul general himself. We were elated!

Upon arrival at the consulate and after multiple security checks, we met a dignified man in his seventies. John detailed my invitation from Rotary International and his three parishes in the US, all eager to support me. The consul general, reviewing my documents, reiterated the initial concerns: I was considered a "flight risk" because I had limited ties compelling my return to Haiti, especially given my age and family circumstances.

John passionately elaborated on my educational background and the hardships that had delayed my schooling, making me older than typical US students. He assured the consul general of his personal commitment to my return after the exchange year. Roger Daley was still not convinced of the validity of John's claims and wanted proof that he was reliable.

Roger requested a second appointment with Gladys Thomas present, also. John, Gladys, and I returned the following day. Gladys had known John and Mary since 1989 when they adopted my two sisters. She had visited with them every summer at the reunions in Minnesota for families with adopted Haitian children, so she had seen first-hand the deep commitment that John and Mary have for their two daughters. Gladys spoke very highly of John and the Lee family.

After careful consideration, the consul general reluctantly approved my J1 visa on September 6, 2000. John and I thanked Roger Daley profusely, then quickly went to Sogebank to pay the $45 required fee for my visa. By 3:30 p.m. we were able to pick it up at the US Consulate.

The elation I felt was indescribable. A once-closed door had opened, bringing me closer to a future brimming with possibilities. I couldn't wait to share the miraculous news with my family!

That evening, we gathered in heartfelt prayer, expressing deep gratitude for John and Mary's unwavering determination—and for God's divine intervention in opening this path. We shared a celebratory meal, and my close friends came to say goodbye. I was overwhelmed by a mix of emotions—joy, anxiety, and a sense of awe at the journey ahead. Stepping into the unknown felt both thrilling and terrifying, but above all, I was excited.

Saying goodbye to my baby nephew, Cleeford, was the hardest part of all. He was only one year old at the time of my departure, and I had been like a second mama to him from the very beginning. I was there the day he was born, and from that moment, we formed a bond that words can't fully describe. Leaving him behind felt like a cruel twist in the midst of such a hopeful journey. Of all the goodbyes, his was the one that broke me the most.

On September 7, John and I traveled to the airport and boarded a DC-3 Missionary Flights International (MFI) plane. Thus I began my journey to the United States of America. MFI is an aviation service that provides transportation and logistical support for missionaries and mission organizations.

CHAPTER 12

Welcome to the United States of America

UPON ARRIVING IN West Palm Beach, Florida, standing next to the US flag, John welcomed me to the United States of America and made a pledge with his right hand over his chest, promising to care for me and ensure my well-being.

Staying in a hotel for the first time felt unbelievable. I marveled at the room that was entirely mine, complete with a soft bed that felt like it had the very highest thread count sheets—not that I was counting. It was a small taste of a world I had only ever longed for. After settling in, John took me out to eat, and on that day, September 7, 2000, my world shifted.

We arrived at Wendy's, and I froze when I saw the menu. The vibrant pictures of burgers, fries, and drinks instantly took me back to a memory from Haiti. Years earlier, I had stumbled upon a similar menu at my mother's workplace. I remember sitting quietly in the corner, staring at the glossy images of food I couldn't name but desperately wished I could taste. At the time, I tried to imagine what it must be like to live like the wealthy, able to order such meals without a second thought. And now, here I was, staring at a similar menu—but this time, it was mine to choose from.

John looked at me and said, "Order whatever you want." His words hit me like a wave. For a moment, I didn't know how to respond. In Haiti, the concept of choosing anything you wanted—without limitations—was inconceivable. Eating out was an indulgence for the privileged, not something for someone like me. I was so overwhelmed, but I held it together. I scanned the menu, carefully choosing items I could somewhat pronounce, wanting to appear as composed as possible.

When the food arrived, it felt like a dream. The meal wasn't extravagant by American standards, but to me, it was everything. I savored every bite, taking my time to enjoy the flavors—something I rarely did back home in Haiti. Food in Haiti was never about enjoyment; it was about survival. As I have said time and time again, living in poverty, food insecurity is a constant companion. Even as you eat, the thought looms: *This is good, but will I eat tomorrow?* That question hangs over every meal, stripping it of joy. You don't have the luxury to savor because your mind is already calculating the next step, the next meal—or the lack thereof.

That day at Wendy's, I experienced something I hadn't truly known before: freedom. For the first time, I wasn't worried about tomorrow. I didn't have to rush through my meal or fear that there wouldn't be another one. I simply enjoyed it, and I felt my past lift, even if just for a little while. The meal was a moment of dignity, of joy, and of hope—a foretaste of a future my friends and I had wished for on the long dusty walks to school, when washing clothes at the river, or while in bed with an aching belly.

After eating, John and I went back to the hotel, and when I got to my room, I turned the TV on CNN. I started watching, trying to understand what the anchor was saying. They spoke so fast; I could barely catch a word. I became frightened, thinking, *Oh my, I thought I knew more English than this.* I realized the little English I knew couldn't even scratch the surface of what awaited me.

I prayed to God that night to help me learn the language quickly. I told Him this opportunity was my ticket out of poverty, but I wasn't sure how I was going to make it in school with the limited English I had. Without mastering English, this chance would be wasted. I pleaded with God, "Please help me do well in my studies." I prayed and believed that God would make a way. He had brought me this far—what my family and I thought was impossible. Things like this didn't happen to people of my background in Haiti. Yet here I was. I prayed and believed God had a plan. Plus, John had promised that he and his family would do anything they could to help me.

I went to sleep, but the excitement of being in this wonderful country—which we described as a land where milk and honey flow—made it hard to rest. So much was running through my mind as I lay in bed in the hotel, knowing that in less than twenty-four hours, I was going to see my sisters.

I wondered how they had changed since they left Haiti eleven years ago. They were the best part of my life growing up, but they had to leave when I was only nine. I cared for them as babies even though we were only six years apart. I rehearsed how I would behave when I saw them. *Would I hug them? Greet them with our traditional Haitian kiss on the cheeks? Would I jump on them? Or would I simply freeze?* I had such a long internal monologue that night. So many questions were going through my mind about that pending reunion. I could barely wait.

On my first morning in a hotel, I remembered my mother's constant advice: "Always clean up after yourself." Determined to uphold her teachings, I meticulously made the bed, ensuring it looked as pristine as when I arrived. Unbeknownst to me, hotel guests typically leave beds unmade upon checkout. It was a humorous realization that, despite my best intentions, I still had much to learn about the customs of this new world.

We had a hearty breakfast at the hotel. It was a buffet-style meal, and again I was stunned by the amount of food before me. John told me I could eat as much as I wanted; the only rule was that I had to get a clean plate every time I returned for more. I couldn't believe what I was hearing!

"You mean I can go more than once?"

"Yes."

"More than twice?"

"Yes."

"More than five times?"

"Yes. As many times as you'd like."

I was overwhelmed. My appetite left me altogether. I started thinking of my family at home and wondered if they had any food that day. Most of the time, the answer was no. Our usual breakfast was coffee and bread. Both were fairly inexpensive. I started having coffee as early as I can remember—perhaps when I was just two years old. That morning in the restaurant, with the abundance of food in front of me, I thought, *What a turn of events.* Just a few days ago, I wondered where my next meal would come from. Oh, life has a sense of humor.

That day, we traveled on American Airlines, and I was in awe of the larger, more sophisticated plane than the one we took from Haiti. When we arrived in Minneapolis, John and Mary's good friend, Sue, picked us up in a beautiful car, the nicest one I'd ever ridden in.

Everyone in the car put on a seatbelt, something I had never used before. I watched them closely, hoping to learn by observing, but when it was time to take it off, I missed seeing how they did it. I struggled for a moment, pressing buttons and pulling at the belt, until I finally heard the "click" and freed myself. It felt like a victory, and I quietly thanked God. I had a lot to learn about this new, sophisticated life in the United States.

Sue drove us to her house, where we were warmly welcomed. She greeted me with a kind hug and handed me a beautiful cloth purse—my very first purse—as a welcome gift to the United

States. It was the first gesture of welcome I had received from someone other than John, and it meant so much. This is such a fond memory for me. After a brief visit with Sue and her husband, we loaded our few bags into John's car and began the last leg of this trip to my new home.

On the drive to Detroit Lakes, John stopped for ice cream—only my second time ever having it in my life. I ordered vanilla. The creamy sweetness felt like a luxury, and I relished each bite. Afterward, we continued on our four-hour drive, and John filled the time by teaching me English words and singing the spelling of "Mississippi" together: "M-I-S-S-I-S-S-I-P-P-I." We sang it over and over, the joy of it lifting my spirits as we journeyed to my new home.

We stopped for dinner in St. Cloud. As we stood in line at the buffet, I noticed a woman glancing at me, her eyes scanning me with a mix of concern and something colder—judgment. Then, under her breath, she muttered something I couldn't quite catch, but John did. I saw him stiffen beside me.

I hesitated before asking, but curiosity and unease won out. "What did she say?"

John exhaled slowly, choosing his words with care. "She said, 'How disgusting to see someone so thin,'" he explained softly, then quickly added, "She probably assumes it's self-inflicted, like an eating disorder."

His words settled over me, heavier than the woman's glance.

I tried to let his words soften the blow, but her judgment cut deeper than I wanted to admit. If only that lady knew. If only she understood the kind of life I had endured in Haiti. Being malnourished wasn't a choice; it was a reality forced upon me. Hunger and parasites had ravaged my body for years, leaving me weak and frail—not because I wanted it, but because I had no other choice.

Her disgust wasn't just directed at my frame; it felt like a dismissal of my story, my struggle, my survival. I wanted to tell her that no one chooses to carry the scars of hunger. I wanted to ask her for grace, for understanding, but instead, I stood there, silent, a wave of emotions crashing inside me. Shame. Anger. Sadness.

I swallowed my pain, as I had done so many times before, and moved forward in line. But her words lingered, a grave reminder of how the stories of people like me—stories of survival, resilience, and struggle—remain unspoken and invisible to the world. How easy it was for her to judge, to dismiss me with a glance, without knowing what I carried. My frail frame told a story she couldn't hear, a truth she couldn't see. And in her ignorance, she made me feel small in a way that hunger never did.

We reached Detroit Lakes around 10 p.m., pulling up to a beautiful white and green colonial house on a quiet street. I marveled at its grandeur as I said to myself, "Miquette, welcome to your new life." Mary greeted us warmly, and I was filled with gratitude as I hugged her.

CHAPTER 13

Sisters

THEN CAME THE moment I had longed for—the moment that had lived in my dreams for eleven long years: reuniting with my sisters, Farah and Cherline. Suddenly, I was in their home, and they were just upstairs, waiting to come down. My heart pounded in my chest.

As I stood down there at the entrance, my breath caught in my throat, listening to the soft shuffle of their feet pacing above me. Their whispers drifted down the stairs like echoes of the past. I could make out their nervous exchange: Farah urging Cherline to go first, and Cherline refusing, saying, "No, you go first." They were unsure—just as unsure as I was—how to step into this long-awaited moment.

They were utterly nervous. But I waited, patient and hopeful. The years of longing had taught me that the best things come to those who wait. No matter how long it took for them to appear, I was ready. Ready to embrace them. Ready to bridge the years that had separated us. Ready to finally feel whole again.

Finally, Mary called them out, "Girls, they're here. Come down now." My breath caught in my chest as I saw them slowly descend the stairs. And then—oh, the joy! The overwhelming, soul-deep joy as my baby sisters, now grown into beautiful young women, came into view. We embraced tightly, the years and distance melting away in an instant.

Tears spilled freely as I held them close, feeling the warmth of their bodies and the strength of their arms around me. I touched their faces, their hair, their hands—anything to convince myself this was real, that they were here, no longer just a memory or a dream. They were no longer the little girls who left Haiti; they were beautiful, poised, speaking a language I wasn't yet fluent in. But in that moment, no words were necessary.

The silence spoke everything we couldn't—years of longing, love, and loss. There was so much I wanted to say, so much to ask, but instead, I let myself soak in the moment. I held them tighter, as if letting go might shatter this fragile, beautiful reality. For now, it was enough just to be together, to feel their presence and their love. It was everything I had waited for, and it was worth every second of the wait.

Mary led me upstairs and opened the door to a room with a warm smile. "This is your room," she said softly. "If you need anything, don't hesitate. Make yourself at home." Her words felt dream-like, as though they belonged to someone else's life, not mine. I stepped inside, stunned. A full-size bed, a closet big enough to hold more than I could ever imagine owning, a desk waiting for dreams to be written, and a carpet so soft it seemed impossible.

That carpet stopped me in my tracks. When I was alone that night, I took off my shoes and curled my toes into its fibers, a sensation so foreign it sent a wave of emotion crashing over me. Back in Port-au-Prince, dirt floors were my reality. We swept them daily to keep the dust at bay, but they remained hard, unyielding, and bare. This carpet, so soft and forgiving under my feet, felt like as if my steps on this hard walk of life were finally experiencing some cushion.

That first night, I couldn't bring myself to sleep in the bed. It was too much, too far from the life I had always known. Instead, I lay on the carpet, pressing my palms and face against it, as if trying to convince myself it was real. For several nights, I chose the floor. I needed time to take it all in, to let the wonder of this place settle in my heart. A room to myself. A bed of my own. A softness I had never known. It was more than comfort—it was hope, wrapped in every thread.

The next morning, Mary called us down to breakfast. The table was beautifully set, every detail carefully arranged, and we gathered around to pray in unison, just as John had taught me in Haiti. The meal was wonderful, and as I ate, I found myself instinctively thinking of saving a bit for later—a habit ingrained from years of scarcity. Mary must have sensed my hesitation because she leaned toward me with a gentle smile and said, "Eat up, Miquette. There'll be plenty of food later." Her words pierced through my thoughts, and a flood of memories washed over me.

I thought of stories my mama had told me, of working at just ten years old in the deputy's house, setting up their grand dining table—a ritual that felt like a world away from our reality. She used to wonder if she or her children would ever experience the sheer joy of partaking in such an act. In our home in Haiti, we never had the privilege of sitting around a table for a meal. There was no dining table, no silverware to share, and no abundance of food to gather over. Meals, when we had them, were eaten wherever we could find a spot, and the idea of sitting together as a family to eat was something we regarded as a luxury meant only for the rich—a distant, unattainable thing.

Yet, like my mama, I still tried to picture what it might be like to live in a home where every meal was shared around a table, surrounded by family, laughter, and love. For some, this may be an ordinary, mundane part of life, but for me, it was one of my biggest dreams—the dream of a poor girl who dared to hope for more.

Now I was living it. For the first time in my life, I didn't worry about food. I could sleep soundly, knowing that tomorrow, I'd have breakfast waiting for me.

Later that day, Mary and John took me shopping. Although I hadn't grown up watching much TV, I'd seen movies like *Clueless*, where characters shopped all the time, and I felt like I was living in one of those scenes. We went to Goodwill first, and I carefully chose bright, flowery clothes. I couldn't believe they paid for it all.

Then we went to JC Penney, which I accidentally called "Jack Penney," making Farah and Cherline burst out laughing. The store was even more beautiful, and Mary told me to pick out whatever I needed—pants, shoes, anything. I was on cloud nine. For the first time, I had more than two undergarments, didn't worry about the next meal, and didn't need to set my sleeping mat in the sun to kill bed bugs. I had a soft bed, a warm family, and security.

The first week in my new home was filled with so many firsts. Some nights, when I thought everyone was asleep, I would tip-toe downstairs to open the fridge and peek inside. I had to see for myself if it was truly full, as John and Mary had assured me. Opening that huge, two-door fridge was surreal. Inside, I found all kinds of fresh food and to my amazement, multiple containers of ice cream. I finally understood what that US consulate officer had meant by calling me a "flight risk." With so many flavors of ice cream, I wasn't sure I'd ever want to leave.

BRIDGING THE GAP

Minnesota was so wildly different from everything I'd known growing up in Haiti. My first experiences as a resident were a mix of awe, confusion, and a whole lot of shivering. Living in the Lees' household with my sisters—who, after more than a decade apart, felt like strangers—was both a gift and a challenge. To understand the complexity, one must first step into their world. Cherline was in eighth grade, Farah had just started her freshman year of high school, and I, at twenty years old, was still in eleventh grade.

Explaining our relationship to others was no easy task. How could Farah and Cherline tell their friends that I was their sister when their American parents were not mine? How could they put into words the tangled web of circumstances that had shaped our lives?

The fact that I was there—that John had actually pulled it off to bring me to the US as a foreign exchange student—was crazy. Cherline once told me about that initial conversation John had with her and Farah where he shared his idea to bring me from Haiti. It had seemed so farfetched, and then she said, "But of course, it's John Lee." His persistence was unmatched.

But my presence there, while a miracle for me, was a reality that didn't fit neatly into any familiar mold, adding yet another layer of complexity to our already delicate household dynamic.

Farah, as a minority in her high school, stood out. She was navigating a world where fitting in and being liked were paramount, and then I showed up. We laugh about it now, but at the time, my presence embarrassed her. Imagine being fifteen years old and introducing your older sister, a twenty-year-old who looked extremely malnourished and awkward. I was so thin that even a size 0 felt too big for me. I was an awkward duck, and Farah's friends—naturally curious—began asking her questions about me. "Is she really your sister?" How does a teenager, desperate to blend into her peer group, answer that?

Despite these challenges, Farah excelled socially and athletically. Her athletic prowess made her popular, even though my arrival was an added complication to her life. I don't blame her for her feelings, but it was hard for me to navigate as well.

While I didn't attend school with Cherline, I went to her and Farah's sports matches, and her friends were equally as curious. Their complimentary assessment of my appearance helped Cherline, as a minority in her school as well, begin to see the beauty in our biological family.

However at home, there was an undercurrent of awkwardness. Passing each other in the hallway often resulted in a hesitant "excuse me." We all longed to know each other better, especially me. As the eldest, I felt a deep desire to bridge the gap and share stories about our family in Haiti, to tell them how much they were loved, and to explain why they were given up for adoption. But there were barriers: the language barrier, the cultural differences, and the lingering awkwardness between us.

I cherished the time I spent with my sisters, but deep down, I wished our relationship could mirror the bonds I had left behind in Haiti with my other siblings. Those relationships were filled with warmth, laughter, fights, and understanding. Here, I found myself praying for time to ease the challenges, but I knew that time was not on my side. I only had one year to build these connections. The thought of leaving with so much left unsaid weighed heavily on me. There were so many emotions, so much history, and so much love I wanted to share, but the words felt trapped within me.

John and Mary did everything they could to nurture a sense of unity between us. Their love and dedication to their children was extraordinary, and I am forever grateful for their efforts. Yet, the adjustment was undeniably difficult for all of us. Things began to shift when John and Mary visited Haiti. But that's a story for later.

During my time with the Lees, I was blessed to gain two more brothers, Carl and Dan. They welcomed me with open arms. Though Dan had already graduated and moved out, it was wonderful to see him during the summer and during the holidays. Carl, who had just started college in Duluth, also made me feel at home.

Carl became my personal benchmark for mastering English. He spoke fast—so fast that his words barely seemed to leave his mouth before the next ones tumbled out. I told myself, *I'll know*

I've truly mastered English when I can understand Carl completely. It became a goal I was determined to achieve. And when that moment finally came, it was exhilarating.

Carl gave up his room for me when I moved in. He had just started college and likely imagined coming home to the familiar comfort of his own space during breaks. Instead, he adapted without complaint, making the basement his home during holidays and even sleeping on the porch beside his pet snake in the summer.

When I thanked him for letting me use his room and apologized for the inconvenience, he responded with characteristic grace: "I honestly didn't even give it a second thought. I just knew you needed a room, and it felt like the right thing to do."

I was also pleased to learn during that time how Farah and Cherline felt about their adopted parents. Farah often talked about how much she appreciated the effort they made to learn about Black culture in order to help them find their identity in an all-Caucasian community.

Adoption was also not new to John's family as he has an adopted sister, so they were well aware of the blessings, as well as the potential challenges. John and Mary knew when they adopted children who were not infants, but toddlers, that they already had life experiences and history. They always thought it was important for Farah and Cherline to know as much as possible about their life story, where they came from, and who was in their immediate family. They wanted the girls to stay connected to Haiti as much as possible and to feel pride in their cultural heritage.

Mary told me once that during college, John spent a semester at Virginia Union University in Richmond. She said, "Since the student body was 99 percent Black, he became immersed in African American culture, history, food, music, clothes, style, and language. It was a time of enlightenment for him, and he now sees that God was preparing him, bridging the gap for the time when he would welcome two new daughters into his family."

John and Mary were both well aware of what has happened in our nation's history when minorities are separated from and made to feel ashamed of their culture and heritage. So, every year, John and Mary took the girls to an annual Haitian reunion where adopted children from Haiti, along with their families, gather from all over the nation to meet and connect with others, learn about the culture, and even learn to speak the native language of Creole.

Mary was also determined to learn how to do the girls' hair. Black hair texture is quite unique, and early on, Mary learned how to condition and braid it—she would spend countless hours braiding their hair extensions. When Farah attended college, many of her Black friends would ask who did her hair, and she was always so proud to tell them it was her mother! They knew she was White and couldn't believe the amazing job she did! Farah once told me, "I feel so blessed to have parents who 'got it' when it came to cultural diversity—it truly showed in how they cared for us."

Their words and the obvious love they shared reassured me that God had heard our prayers and provided them with the best family we could have prayed for.

CHAPTER 14
Detroit Lakes High School

ON SEPTEMBER 11, 2000, John and Mary dropped me off at Detroit Lakes High School (DLHS), home of the "Lakers," but John stayed with me for the day to help me navigate my new environment and get familiar with school life in America. I could hardly believe that the massive, beautiful structure before me was actually a school. The hallways seemed endless, stretching far in every direction, each leading to another just as long. Rows of storage spaces, which I soon learned were called "lockers," lined the walls, each assigned to a student to store their belongings. I was given my own locker with a combination lock—something completely new to me. I struggled with it for days, unable to figure out the lock, so I simply carried my things around instead until I figured it out.

Each classroom was spacious and well-equipped with supplies—an incredible contrast to my experience in Haiti, where we stayed in the same classroom all day. Here, I had to move from class to class, each subject taught by a different teacher, with its own dedicated textbook.

I will never forget my first day in social studies class with Mrs. Kotschevar. Of course, she knew about my arrival before I stepped into her classroom. That fall, the administration had gathered all the teachers and told them they were getting a new student from Haiti. They knew that my English was not good, and I had had intermittent schooling, so they met to decide which classes to put me in. It was decided I would be in Mrs. Kotschevar's class and

Barb Oistad's American History/English 10 classes. These classes were designed for tenth grade students who were struggling.

On that first day, Mrs. Kotschevar instructed her students to pick up their textbooks from the back of the room. I hesitated, unsure of what to do as my classmates eagerly grabbed their books. Embarrassed and confused, I approached her after class and quietly explained, "I didn't bring any money to buy the book."

Her response left me stunned: "Miquette, you don't have to pay for books. They're free."

I couldn't believe it. "For all of my classes?" I asked in disbelief.

She smiled and said, "Yes, for all of your classes."

By the end of that week, my bag was heavy with books—a weight I carried proudly. For the first time in my life, I had every single school supply I needed for an entire year. Being in these classes opened my eyes to the opportunities offered in school in the United States. For me, I wasn't just carrying books; I was carrying privilege, opportunity, and a profound realization of how little I had back in Haiti. The contrast was overwhelming—and I began to grasp just how much I had been missing all along.

Later on, Mrs. Kotschevar said to me, "It was fun to see you learn. You could literally see the light in your eyes when something came together for you and you understood a word or concept. It is fun to teach those who love to learn." She continued, "I would not have believed it if you had told me in September what you would be able to do in May."

Another teacher who left a lasting impression on me was Mrs. Welke, my biology teacher. I was thrilled to be in a class with its own fully equipped lab. The excitement of seeing microorganisms under a microscope or dissecting fetal pigs was beyond anything I had imagined. This hands-on learning brought education to life—again, such a stark contrast to my experiences in Haiti, where we primarily memorized facts and visualized reactions in our minds without the benefit of practical, hands-on experiences.

One afternoon, as I adjusted my heavy bag filled with books, I thought back to my life in Haiti. There, going to school was a constant struggle, and even basic supplies like pencils were hard to come by. I remembered how my friends and I would gather at the end of each school day to share books, carefully copying notes and lessons since none of us had access to a full set of textbooks. Life in Haiti was challenging, but being a student in poverty was especially brutal. The burden of not having enough resources weighed on our dreams.

DLHS had so many amenities I never imagined could be part of a school: a swimming pool, gym, teacher and staff lounges, and most impressively, a huge cafeteria.

The adjustment was overwhelming, not only because of the language barrier but also because I found myself in an all-Caucasian city for the very first time. Everywhere I went—classrooms, stores, church pews—I stood out. I wasn't just *new*. I was visibly *different*. I felt exposed in a way that went deeper than skin. People were kind but often unsure of how to relate. I could feel the unspoken questions, the polite distance. I longed for the ease of cultural familiarity, for a space where I could just belong without explanation.

In the classroom, the challenges multiplied. My teachers spoke quickly, using phrases and methods that were completely new to me. I had to work twice as hard just to keep up—not only translating the language but trying to decode the culture behind it. It was exhausting. But I loved the fact that homework counted toward my final grade. In Haiti, homework was merely preparation for exams and didn't contribute to our final marks. Here, I could use homework to bolster my overall grade, and I took every extra-credit opportunity my teachers offered.

There were also so many extra-curricular activities available. Back in Haiti, singing had always been my escape, my way of coping. When life felt overwhelming, I would sing my heart out—sometimes to the point where I forgot I was hungry. In a way, music turned my grumbling stomach into a melody.

So, when I found out I could join the choir, I was over the moon. I absolutely loved being part of the choir. It was led by the wonderful Mrs. Larson, who had the kind of patience you'd expect from someone dealing with a group of kids trying to harmonize but often just yelling at different pitches.

For me, choir practice was like finding a piece of home. Standing there with everyone, belting out notes that occasionally hit the right pitch, I felt like I belonged. It wasn't just about the music— it was about the joy of losing yourself in a song, of letting your voice carry you to a place where worries didn't matter. It was the first time in a long while that I sang just for the love of it, not to make time or hunger disappear.

CHALLENGES

One of the other things I loved at DLHS was gym class. In the first week, we were encouraged to challenge ourselves with weightlifting. Determined to make an impression, I eagerly did reps and squats, pushing myself to the limit. The other students seemed impressed, and of course, I showed off a little. But I paid for it. The next day, every muscle in my body ached, and I couldn't even make it down the stairs without screaming in pain. Mary took one look at me and decided I wasn't going to school that day. Missing even one day of school felt like I was wasting time. I prayed to stay healthy, to not let anything pull me from class. I didn't want to miss a single lesson, especially because my mind held onto information best through the stories teachers shared. Those stories helped me build a bridge between this world and my own past, where school was a constant struggle.

Frustrated with myself for overdoing it in gym class, I learned to pace myself.

Sports at DLHS were an unforgettable part of my American high school experience. Farah and Cherline were both incredibly active, excelling in track and field, soccer, and a range of other sports. Watching them compete was thrilling, yet it stirred something bittersweet within me. I couldn't help but wonder, *What if I had been given the same opportunities back home? Would I have been just as strong, just as confident?* Their dedication and skill filled me with admiration—and a tinge of longing for a chance that I never had. I saw how sports empowered them and gave them confidence, and I wondered what it might feel like to be part of a team, to feel that rush of competition. The dreams of what could've been lingered as I sat in the stands, cheering them on.

Attending football games with my host family was another experience entirely. The energy in the stands was electric, the crowd's chants and cheers reverberating around the stadium, filling the crisp air with life. I loved every second of it. These moments made me feel like I was truly part of something larger, like I belonged.

Volunteering at the concession stand was my way of contributing, of being part of the school community, and it also gave me the precious chance to practice my English. One particular day still sticks with me—a day that highlighted the quirks of this new language I was learning.

A student came up to the counter and asked to purchase a "Three Musketeers." I smiled, wanting to help and eager to make a good impression. I didn't know "Three Musketeers" was the name of a single candy bar, so I promptly handed him three individual Musketeer bars. The student chuckled and said, "Oh, no, I only need one Three Musketeers!" I looked at him, completely baffled, and replied, "But that's what I gave you—three Musketeers!"

In that moment, laughter erupted from everyone around. They tried to explain that "Three Musketeers" was just one candy bar, not three separate ones. I felt my cheeks flush with embarrassment, but I joined in their laughter, too. It was a humbling yet heartwarming experience—a reminder that even though I was still learning, I was surrounded by people who found joy in the little misunderstandings, who accepted me, who cared enough to laugh with me and not at me. This small moment showed me the warmth of the people around me and how this strange new language, with all its quirks, was slowly becoming mine.

I will never forget the countless hours John and Mary patiently poured into helping me with my homework. Math and writing were particularly difficult for me. Back in Haiti, I'd never written more than half a page for any assignment, and now, in this new world, I was expected to write pages upon pages—three, sometimes six or more. I struggled to organize my thoughts, let alone express them in English. John and Mary spent night after night helping me outline ideas and guiding me through each sentence, as I wrestled to understand what seemed impossible.

The first challenge, though, was learning to type. I had never used a computer before. The only time I'd been near one, I managed to touch a single key when no one was looking, wondering what it could possibly mean to have all those letters lined up on a machine. It seemed miraculous how Farah and Cherline typed with such ease, especially Farah, who typed so quickly she didn't even need to look at the keyboard. I marveled at her, as if she were performing magic. I took a computer class, but while my classmates' fingers flew, I was painstakingly searching for each letter, lost and overwhelmed. My teacher was patient, and John and Mary encouraged me to practice on their desktop every evening. Each time I typed just a little faster, they cheered for me, and those small cheers fed my spirit.

At my new school, many students were curious about me. They asked questions about Haiti, my family, and my life. When they asked my age, I told them I was twenty. Most didn't seem to care, but one boy—whom we will name Tim—saw it as an opportunity to mock me relentlessly. Every day, he made it his mission to remind everyone about the "twenty-year-old in school."

One day in biology, a substitute teacher was taking attendance, calling each student by name. When he got to mine, Tim seized his moment and shouted, "SHE'S TWENTY!" The whole class turned to stare. My heart sank, my face burned, and I wished I could disappear.

I couldn't understand why my age seemed so wrong here. In Haiti, school wasn't always linear—we attended when we could, often finishing in our mid- to late-twenties if we were fortunate enough to stay in school at all. But in that moment, none of that mattered. I felt exposed, small, and out of place in a way I never had before.

The boy's laughter echoed in my mind for days, and his whispers seemed to follow me down every hall. But I couldn't let him distract me, not when I'd come this far. I made a plan: The second the bell rang, I would slip to the back of the room, walk home during the warmer months, or be the first on the bus when winter set in. I would outmaneuver his cruelty with quiet resilience.

My whole life, poverty tried to silence my voice, but I refused to let it win. And now, more than ever, I had been given a golden opportunity—one that most children in my home country could only dream of. I was the lucky one, and nothing—not even his words—could take that away from me.

On October 4, 2000, Mary took me to get a physical and the required vaccinations for school, and the reality of my past clung to me once more, even in the sterile, clinical setting of the doctor's office. The notes the doctor wrote about me—a few short sentences—captured more than just my current health. They reflected the reality of a life shaped by poverty and deprivation:

"Twenty-year-old female presents to the clinic for regular healthcare maintenance. She is a foreign student living in the Detroit Lakes area for the current school term. She was from a family with no preventative healthcare maintenance. She was malnourished upon arrival. She is currently taking a multivitamin. She has gained 10+ pounds since arrival in the last six weeks."

As I read those words, my mind drifted to my sister, Keke. She was beautiful, full of life, and so much more than her too-short years allowed her to show the world. When Keke fell ill, there was no doctor to call, no clinic to visit, no medication to ease her pain. We watched helplessly as the fever consumed her. And when she was gone, we mourned her with the hollow understanding that her death wasn't inevitable; it was the cruel outcome of poverty's grip on our lives. Keke died from a fever that might have been treatable—if only she had good healthcare. But she never had. The thought still aches in my chest: a simple fever, and yet, it stole her life. Then my mind shifted to the brother I never had the chance to meet because he died from malnutrition at just two and half years old.

For people like us in Haiti, access to medical care wasn't just limited; it was non-existent. Healthcare wasn't something you planned for—it was a luxury.

Sitting there in the clinic, I couldn't shake the contrast. Here I was, going to school, having regular meals, receiving care, gaining weight, being given the chance to reclaim my health. But my sister Keke and brother Wilfrid never had that chance. Their lives, dreams, potential—all lost to a system that failed to see them as deserving of care.

CHAPTER 15

Firsts

WHILE IN DETROIT LAKES, I experienced many "firsts" that left a lasting impression. John and Mary were determined to give me the best year of my life and expose me to as many adventures as possible.

John was a pastor of not just one but three churches in the Detroit Lakes area, a role that was as demanding as it was inspiring. Each church had its own unique congregation, its own rhythm and spirit, but John moved between them seamlessly, bringing his warmth, guidance, and commitment to each.

When I first arrived, he brought me to all three churches—Bakke, Lund, and Richwood. He introduced me to each congregation as if I were part of his own family. The members were incredibly welcoming, and although I didn't understand everything being said, I could feel their warmth and kindness. John's sermons were captivating. He had a way of weaving stories and lessons together that made everyone feel like he was speaking directly to them, addressing their lives, their struggles, and their hopes.

As I became more involved, I started to read Scripture at each of his churches, a task that filled me with both pride and nervousness. I practiced reading the passages in English over and over, determined to pronounce each word correctly, especially those that were unfamiliar to me. Standing in front of each congregation with John's steady encouragement behind me was a powerful experience. It made me feel not only welcomed but also valued—like I was part of something bigger than myself. These churches became a second home and their members, a second family. It was incredibly healing to know my sisters grew up in this atmosphere.

In the fall of 2000, John invited me to attend a Pow Wow at White Earth, one of the largest Indian reservations in Minnesota. A Pow Wow is a sacred Native American gathering that celebrates culture through drumming, singing, and traditional dances, each carrying deep spiritual and historical significance. The experience was mesmerizing—the vibrant colors, rhythmic drumbeats, and deep cultural pride reminded me so much of home.

As I watched the dancers move in harmony with the music, I couldn't help but draw parallels to Haitian traditions, especially our *Rara* rituals. Both celebrations use music, movement, and storytelling to honor ancestors and preserve cultural identity. Witnessing this was a powerful reminder that, despite our different histories, the spirit of resilience, celebration, and community is universal.

Wherever we went, we usually took John's truck. His vehicle of choice was a Toyota T-100 stick-shift pickup truck with the license plate proudly reading "Tet Bef"—a nickname Haitians often give to SUVs and big cars. It was a fitting name because that truck had a personality all its own.

One day, we were driving from Moorhead after a meeting. As usual, John was multitasking: navigating the road, chatting with me, and sneaking in a few English lessons. It was one of his favorite things to do—helping me expand my vocabulary every chance he got.

Halfway home, John decided it was time for a different kind of lesson: driving. He pulled into a church parking lot, which conveniently also had a cemetery (foreshadowing?). With a big grin, he said, "Okay, your turn to drive!"

Now, mind you, I had been in the US for only one month at that point—I didn't even know how to put on a seatbelt when I first arrived. I stared at him, horrified. *Was he serious?* He handed me the wheel, and I reluctantly slid into the driver's seat.

"Just press the pedal lightly," John instructed. I nodded, panicked, and immediately floored the gas pedal. The truck screeched and bolted forward like it had been shot out of a cannon. John yelled, "PUMP THE BRAKES!" and I, in pure terror, yelled back, "WHAT'S A BRAKE?!"

In the chaos, John reached over, yanked my foot off the gas, and the truck came to a lurching, violent stop, just short of a tall granite gravestone. We sat there in silence, hearts racing, staring out the windshield. The "Tet Bef" had survived, and so had we. Barely. What could have been a headline-worthy disaster is now a story we laugh about. But let's just say John didn't offer me another driving lesson anytime soon. I like how Lynn Hummel, the author of *One Step Forward* put it: "The departed were turning over in their graves."[2]

My first days as a resident of Minnesota were equal parts fascinating and overwhelming, but nowhere was that more evident than my visit to a performance of the Detroit Lakes High School Fall Musical at Roosevelt Middle School.

The auditorium left me completely stunned. Rows of plush seats stretched out like royalty's throne room—so soft and luxurious I half-expected a bill just for sitting down. The stage lights sparkled like something out of a Broadway dream and the sound system? Let's just say it was a far cry from the only "sound system" I knew back home in Haiti—the roosters crowing at dawn.

When the speakers roared to life, I nearly jumped out of my seat, convinced the building itself was performing. It felt like I'd stumbled onto the set of one of those glamorous movies I'd only caught glimpses of growing up. As I sat there, surrounded by

---

[2] Hummel, Lynn. *One Step Forward: The Story of TeacHaiti's School of Hope*, 2014, p. 54.

dazzling lights and booming sound, I couldn't shake the feeling that I'd stepped into a whole new universe—one where magic and possibilities were just part of everyday life.

Coming out of the performance, I stepped outside to head to the car when I noticed these white, fluffy things falling from the sky. I froze, eyes wide open, completely mesmerized. I tilted my head back, enchanted by the sparkling blanket covering everything, and, naturally, I did what any curious soul would do—I stuck out my tongue to catch a snowflake. As it melted, I laughed like a kid discovering candy for the first time.

But let me tell you, the joy didn't last long. Moments later, I realized something crucial: Snow isn't just pretty—it's cold. Painfully, unforgivably cold. The kind of cold that makes you question every life choice that led to you standing outside, pretending to enjoy winter. Let's just say my honeymoon phase with snow was over in record time.

Then there were the Minnesota staples: sledding, ice skating, and trying not to fall on icy sidewalks. From the moment I stepped foot in that snowy wonderland, it felt like I was part of some winter survival reality show that I hadn't signed up for. But John and Mary were determined to make sure I experienced it all. Skiing? A mix of sheer terror and exhilaration as I hurtled down a hill, praying I wouldn't crash into a tree. Ice skating? Let's just say I spent more time on the ice than on my skates. But they cheered me on, convinced I was "embracing" winter, while I secretly counted down the days to spring.

My first Christmas in the US was pure magic—in the best way possible. Growing up in Haiti, Christmas was all about family and food. Every parent tried to make it special, maybe with a doll, a new dress, or a good meal. My parents always did their best, but there just wasn't enough money to go around for toys. So, while I cherished the love and togetherness, the idea of a stack of gifts under a tree was something I'd only seen in movies.

But then came my first American Christmas, and let me tell you—it was a game-changer. The weeks leading up to the holiday felt like the winter season might actually be worth the cold. John and Mary transformed their home into something straight out of a Christmas card. The house was cozy and festive, with twinkling lights strung outside and a beautifully decorated tree inside. It wasn't the giant, movie-style tree, but to me, it was the most magical thing I'd ever seen.

We all worked together to decorate it, hanging ornaments and stringing lights. At the base of the tree, a little train circled around on a track. I was completely mesmerized by that train, watching it go round and round like it was performing just for me. And then there were the presents. So many presents. I'd never seen anything like it—a sea of colorful, shiny packages under the tree. I didn't even know where to look first.

Mary made sure the holiday was about more than just decorations. She prepared special meals, including her favorite oyster stew served in her best china on Christmas Eve. I didn't even know what an oyster was, but I ate it like it was the best thing I'd ever tasted. The whole house smelled amazing, and the anticipation of Christmas morning had me too excited to sleep.

When the big day finally came, I jumped out of bed at the first hint of daylight. We rushed downstairs, greeted by the smell of Mary's warm breakfast, and gathered in the living room for the main event: gift-opening time.

It was a whole system. Each gift was labeled with someone's name, and we took turns opening them one by one. The suspense was almost unbearable. When it was finally my turn, I tore into the wrapping paper, and there it was—my very own radio that could play CDs. But wait—it got better. Alongside it was a Céline Dion CD. Let me tell you, I spent the rest of that day belting out "My Heart Will Go On" like I was headlining a concert.

There were plenty of other gifts, but that radio and CD? They were everything. I'll never forget the feeling of holding something so special in my hands, wrapped in festive paper, with my name on it.

The laughter and joy we shared as a family that day made it all the more unforgettable. The experience wasn't just about the gifts—it was about the love, the thoughtfulness, and the sense of belonging. It left me in awe, and I made a silent vow to myself: One day, I'd recreate that kind of Christmas magic for my own family.

CHAPTER 16

Borrowed Time

MY TIME IN Detroit Lakes was one of the most transformative years of my life. I learned and absorbed so much during those twelve months. One of the highlights was the Rotary Youth Exchange celebration, where all the exchange students in the district gathered in Duluth for a weekend of fun and connection. It was incredible meeting students from all over the world.

As part of the celebration, students were invited to participate in a talent show. Those with obvious talents were brimming with excitement. I, on the other hand, was filled with dread. *I have no talent,* I told myself. My good friend Ai from Japan was a phenomenal piano player; others played guitar, danced, or showcased unique skills. I racked my brain, searching for something—anything—I could do.

Then it hit me. I would do what I had done countless times back home in Haiti: balance a big bucket of water on my head. It may not have been flashy, but it was uniquely me. So that's exactly what I did. To my surprise, it was a hit. I also sang Haiti's national anthem, and the warm applause that followed filled me with pride. Seeing their joy made me feel proud, too. For a moment, I realized that even the simplest things from my everyday life back home could be seen as extraordinary.

In the few months leading to the end of my chapter there, I started thinking about returning home and what it would be like. I found myself battling emotions I didn't know how to process. I loved my home. I loved my family. The thought of going back to see them filled me with joy. I missed them deeply. But something in me had changed. I had been exposed to a new way of living, and I couldn't unsee it. For the first time, I understood that there is a basic standard of life every human being should have—not just a privilege for the few.

I had experienced access to uninterrupted education without the fear of being sent home for unpaid tuition, food that was always available, a bed of my own, a quiet space to do homework, and most importantly, a place where dreams flourish and come true. I experienced all of that while living with the Lees. But I knew—I was on borrowed time.

And nothing back home had changed. My parents still shared one small room where six to eight of us crowded in at night. There was still no plumbing. Still no running water. Electricity was only available for a few hours a day—and sometimes, there was none at all. Every day was a battle to survive. The noise, the chaos, the uncertainty of daily life—it was all still there, familiar and waiting for me.

The idea of going back permanently—without having accomplished my dream—felt unbearably heavy. It wasn't just about comfort; it was about purpose.

That big dream of becoming a nurse had begun to feel possible in Minnesota. I couldn't stop thinking about it. I didn't want to let it go. I had carried it for so long, and now, it felt closer than ever—like it could be the very catalyst that would change the trajectory of my life and ultimately, my family's. I didn't want to go back to living the way I had before moving there. I wanted so badly to keep going, to stay and build on what had begun in Minnesota.

But the Rotary and the Lees had done their part. They had given me the gift of a year—an extraordinary, life-altering year. And that was the deal. I had made a promise to return home, and I intended to honor that promise.

I prayed desperately that God would make a way, that He would give me the tools to continue this journey. I knew the road ahead wouldn't be easy. Going back to not having indoor plumbing would not be pleasant! My dream would take more time, more education, more opportunities—things that felt out of reach. But I forced myself to snap out of the sorrow of the inevitable and chose, instead, to be grateful. I had experienced something extraordinary, and I clung to that with everything in me. I resolved to use this experience to the best of my ability—to carve a new path, no matter how hard it would be.

How that was going to happen, I had no idea. I thanked God and prayed He would make a way. And He did.

During the summer of 2001, right before I was set to return to Haiti, John and Mary told me they discovered there was a way for me to return to the US to continue my education!

They immediately began brainstorming ways to secure the necessary funding. With less than two weeks before I had to leave for Haiti, the urgency was immense. They explored the possibility of my attending Oak Grove Lutheran High School in Fargo, North Dakota. It would still be expensive at $8,000 to $10,000, but it was a more feasible option than staying at Detroit Lakes, which required $13,000 in tuition.

They say it takes a village to raise a child, but I've learned that sometimes it takes a global community to rewrite a future. My journey is a testament to that truth. Whenever I faced what seemed like an insurmountable challenge, extraordinary people stepped up, proving that compassion and determination can overcome even the greatest obstacles.

Determined to make it happen, John and Mary explored every possible avenue, rallying support and seeking solutions to ensure I wouldn't lose this opportunity.

John decided to approach the Detroit Lakes Noon Rotary Club again—the same club that had originally brought me to the US. He knew they were already familiar with my story: growing up in abject poverty, defying the odds, and thriving during my time in Detroit Lakes. If anyone would be moved to take action, he believed it would be them.

John shared the urgent need for funding, emphasizing how close I was to continuing my education in the US and the impact it could have on my future. He knew that Rotary's mission aligned with creating opportunities for young people like me, and he hoped their generosity would once again open a door that might otherwise remain closed.

During the club's "Happy Dollars" tradition, John requested to speak. He was granted less than sixty seconds, but that was all he needed. Standing before the club, he passionately made the case:

"Miquette is leaving in less than two weeks to return to Haiti. The good news is that she can come back right away to start her education at Oak Grove. The bad news is we need $8,000 in less than two weeks to cover her tuition. How can you help?"

It was a bold and heartfelt request, but John is a determined man. To his amazement, hands began to shoot up across the room. Members started pledging $250, $500, $1,000—one after another. Before his sixty seconds were up, over $6,000 had been raised. John and Mary pledged to cover the remainder of my expenses at Oak Grove that year.

The club later shared that it was their most successful fundraiser ever accomplished in such a short time. The energy and generosity in the room were truly overwhelming. Through John's determination and the Rotary Club's steadfast support, they enabled me to gather the necessary documents and financial proof to present to the US Consulate in Haiti, with the hope of securing another student visa.

With the tuition to Oak Grove secured, the next step was to return to Haiti. John and Mary had already decided months earlier that they would accompany me back to Haiti. My time in Detroit Lakes had inspired them all to finally make the journey to their daughters' homeland. They felt it was essential for Farah and Cherline to meet their birth parents face-to-face. What better opportunity than my return home?

I asked Mary whether she had thought much about taking the girls to visit Haiti before this, and she said to me in her sweet way, "We've always wanted to connect the girls to their Haitian heritage and your family because that's their story—that's who they are. But we wanted to do a trip when they were old enough to fully understand, appreciate, and embrace the experience."

John and Mary were determined to make the trip unforgettable. Their vision reached beyond my journey home to secure another visa; it encompassed something deeply significant for their own family.

I did my best to prepare them for the trip. I finally shared stories about our family, the circumstances that led to their daughters' adoption, and the deep pain their absence had left behind. I couldn't wait for them to meet my family and witness the dynamics that shaped our lives.

Farah and Cherline had known their birth parents only through fragments of stories, faded childhood memories, and what I shared with them during the year I lived with their family. They had been so young when they left Haiti—just three and three-and-a-half years old. The thought of returning was both daunting and profound. This trip wasn't just about a reunion for Farah and Cherline—it was a journey of self-discovery, an opportunity to reclaim parts of themselves they had long tucked away.

Plane tickets were booked for the five of us: John, Mary, Farah, Cherline, and me. Every detail seemed perfectly planned. But just days before our departure, Cherline approached Mary with tearful eyes and a heartfelt request: She wanted her older brothers, Dan and Carl, to come, too.

Mary listened intently, moved by the emotion behind Cherline's words. She immediately picked up the phone and called John at his office. Her voice carried both urgency and resolve as she explained Cherline's request.

"She really wants her brothers to come, John," Mary said. "This means so much to her."

John paused. "What is this going to cost?" he asked, thinking practically. "Are there even any seats left?"

Despite his initial hesitation, John understood the significance of this journey and the courage behind Cherline's request. "Check with the airline," he said finally.

Mary called the MFI office, explaining the situation. The staff managed to find two extra seats for the flights to and from Port-au-Prince. She then checked with American Airlines, and they could also fit in two more passengers on the flights from Minneapolis to West Palm Beach and back.

Next, Mary reached out to Dan and Carl to see if they were even available. Both brothers were eager to join, though they had to clear the trip with their employers. Luckily, they were able to leave their summer jobs early.

With the flights secured and the logistics settled, the trip was officially a "go" for all seven of us.

Now that there was a chance to secure a new visa, going home stirred a mix of emotions I could barely put into words. The thought that everything could change for me in a matter of days was thrilling—but it also came with a heaviness. It was excitement wrapped in anxiety, layered with hope, fear, and uncertainty.

I couldn't ignore the stakes. If I got the visa, my life would change forever. Becoming a nurse would no longer just be a dream—it would be *possible*. But if the visa wasn't granted, I would stay behind and return to the life I had left—the life of daily struggle, scarcity, and deferred dreams. That tension sat quietly in my chest, always there.

Still, I tried to push those thoughts aside. This trip was monumental for a different reason. My two sisters, Farah and Cherline, were about to meet their birth family for the first time since they left Haiti as toddlers. Now well into their teens, it was time for that long-awaited reunion. The joy, the nerves, the significance of that moment—it all deserved my full presence. So instead of getting lost in my own uncertainty, I focused on them. I focused on the beauty of that reunion and let it anchor me through the storm of emotions stirring inside.

CHAPTER 17
The Trip of a Lifetime

ON AUGUST 8, 2001, we drove to Minneapolis-St. Paul International Airport and flew to West Palm Beach, where we spent the night.

The next day, August 9, we boarded the plane to Port-au-Prince. The excitement and nerves were palpable. Farah and Cherline were stepping into a past they barely remembered, no doubt grappling with profound questions.

On the plane ride, I wondered how Farah and Cherline felt at that moment—on their way to their home country. I watched Farah and Cherline look out of the plane window and peer down as we flew over the majestic mountains, little towns, and farmlands. Did they feel wonder? Angst? Curiosity? Euphoria?

The magnitude of the journey became clear when we finally stood together in Port-au-Prince as a family. All seven of us were united by love, curiosity, and the significance of what was unfolding.

The moment we exited the airport, a wave of emotions hit me. My family stood waiting—my mama, my big brother Pidens, my sisters Sandra and Beatrice—each face carrying years of longing and love. I watched as Farah met our mama. My mother's joy was so abundant, and I could tell Farah was trying to hold in all the emotions to avoid falling apart.

Hugs and smiles filled the space between all of us, bridging the time and distance that had kept us apart. Laughter mixed with joyful tears, and for a moment, the chaos of the airport melted away. But time was not on our side—we had to move quickly.

John, Pidens, and I rushed to Sogebank—the only bank authorized to process payments for US Consulate appointments. The drive alone could take anywhere from fifteen minutes to an hour, depending on traffic. But once you arrived, the real wait began. Bank lines in Haiti are notoriously unpredictable—sometimes just five minutes, other times stretching into five hours. It's wild. Thankfully, when we arrived, the line was manageable, and we were able to complete our transaction in under an hour. The fee at the time was $45—a fraction of what it costs now, over $185.

While we handled the payment, we had left the rest of the Lee family with my family—a well-intentioned but, in hindsight, completely impractical decision. No one in my family spoke English, and no one in the Lee family spoke Creole. What followed was a painfully awkward symphony of silence, stolen glances, and polite, uncomfortable smiles.

When we returned to the airport, Mary looked visibly relieved. Later, she confessed, "I wasn't anxious—except at the airport when you, John, and Pidens left us. That's when I felt vulnerable, trying to watch the girls, afraid someone might take them."

Outside the airport, the scene was alive with movement and color. The arrival area teemed with people—some anxiously scanning the crowd for familiar faces, others simply drawn by the energy, watching as travelers spilled out of the terminal. Then, there were those hoping to earn a few coins, weaving through the crowd and asking for help.

Nearby, a street performer with a puppet worked the crowd, his dancing doll jerking and twirling in an effort to entertain and, more importantly, earn some cash. At first, it was amusing—a lighthearted distraction from the intensity of the moment. But soon, the dance took a turn, the movements becoming … well, less than appropriate. I shifted uncomfortably, hoping he would move on, but he was determined to keep our attention.

Finally, I handed him some money, hoping it would be enough to send him on his way. He took it with a grin, nodded in thanks, and for a brief moment, disappeared into the sea of people. I sighed in relief. But just as I turned back to my family, there he was again—puppet in full swing, even bolder than before.

"Dude, I gave you money to leave. Why are you back?" I asked, caught between annoyance and amusement. Flashing a grin, he replied, "I did leave, didn't I?" I had to laugh—he had a point. I gave him a bit more money and added firmly this time, "Please don't come back." He smiled, nodded, and finally, the puppet show came to an end. Even that moment spoke volumes about the resourcefulness and resilience of the Haitian people—finding creative ways to survive and connect. Beyond the initial awkwardness and hilarious language attempts, our time in Haiti was a blessing none of us could have predicted, filled with memories and emotions and simple joys that made us feel like family.

My father, the one who had struggled the most with the decision to let go when my sisters were adopted, finally found peace. It was written in every line on his face as he looked at Farah and Cherline. He studied their faces, their laughter, their kindness, thanking God for the chance to see them once more—a miracle he never thought he'd see.

Our days were spent sharing stories, meals, and precious time together. We met with extended family, too—aunts, uncles, cousins, nieces, nephews, and neighbors. There were many rooftop conversations late into the evening when it was cool. All of us really bonded during those times. Laughter and tears blended into a tapestry of moments none of us would soon forget.

Cherline believes that trip marked a turning point in our relationship. The awkward moments we experienced back in Detroit

Lakes were long gone. She noticed the natural dynamic between my siblings and me—the ease we had around each other. She later said, "Going to Haiti together was when things shifted. You were the sole connection between us all—the Lees and our Haitian family. Seeing you in your element as a leader was impressive, and I began to realize how amazing and special it is that we had you to fill in the gaps in our adoption story."

But we were also there for another purpose. The day of our appointment at the US consulate had arrived: August 14, 2001. Every breath felt heavy with anticipation. John, Mary, and I were a bundle of nerves, the possibility pressing down on us. They had encouraged me to bring my report cards and a photo album, small but powerful artifacts of my journey—proof of my dedication, my potential, and my unwavering hope for a future.

As we neared the entrance, my heart pounded. Then, suddenly—halt. Security guards blocked our path, their expressions unreadable. My stomach twisted.

John, steady and resolute, stepped forward. In a calm but firm voice, he explained the consul general's promise to see me upon my return to the country. The words hung in the air like a fragile thread holding my fate. The silence that followed was unbearable. Seconds stretched into eternity as they checked our story.

Then, at last—a nod. Permission granted.

As we stepped inside, a wave of relief washed over me. It wasn't victory, not yet. But it was something—a door opening, a small but undeniable step forward.

Sitting in the consul general's office was like revisiting a battlefield. This was where, a year earlier, my hopes had first been crushed. Yet now, I sat there again, stronger, with more to show. We thanked Consul General Roger Daley, and with trembling hands, I passed over my report card. To most, it would have been a simple piece of paper, but to me, it was the embodiment of late nights, of painstaking work in a language still foreign to me. It was my heart on display—mostly As and one B—a testimony to everything I had overcome and poured into this opportunity. Every grade was a reminder of how badly I wanted to prove myself worthy of this chance.

I hoped he would understand—that he would see beyond the grades and recognize the desperation, the hunger for change, embedded in every word. My journey was about so much more than academics. In moments like this, I realized how much I carried with me the hopes of everyone who believed that someone from my background could break free. I was determined to let my voice speak louder than ever, through courage, resilience, and purpose. Consul General Roger Daley was pleased with my accomplishments but also relieved that I had kept my promise to return to Haiti.

John spoke up next, explaining that I needed another student visa to pursue my dream of becoming a nurse—a dream that could transform not only my life but also the lives of others. I handed over my new I-20 form from Oak Grove Lutheran School, along with letters from my supporters in the US—proof of a community that believed in me, that wanted to see me succeed and rise above poverty's grip.

The ambassador examined each document in silence. Every second felt like an eternity. Each page he turned seemed to echo in the room, holding my future hostage.

Finally, he looked up. His gaze was steady but hesitant. "I can only grant this visa if I am certain that, when you return to Haiti, you'll have a job waiting for you."

My heart sank. But John, ever persistent, suggested we reach out to Gladys once more. She had played a pivotal role in my journey, and as the executive director of her own hospital in Port-au-Prince, she would have the influence to convince the consul general that I would have a job waiting for me.

We agreed to return for a second appointment. We contacted Gladys, explained the situation, and without hesitation, she agreed to help. At our second appointment, she sat beside us, looked the consul general in the eye, and assured him that she would gladly offer me a job when I return.

Consul General Roger Daley studied her for a long moment, then shifted his gaze back to me. His expression softened, balancing between reluctance and something else. Finally, he nodded and granted me the F-1 visa.

Two days after our meeting with the consul general, I held my passport in my hands, staring at the most significant stamp I had ever seen. An F-1 visa.

August 16 is forever printed in my mind as the date my life had been given a real future. This small stamp was a doorway I had been pushing to get to my whole life. In that moment, I felt the countless prayers, the dreams whispered and held close. Tears threatened to spill as I realized that I held in my hands not just permission to study but the collective dreams of my family, my community, and everyone who had sacrificed so I could stand here, in this life-changing moment.

When I returned home and shared the news, my family erupted in joy, their voices filling the air with laughter and tears. They circled around me, laying hands on me as they had done so many times before, praying for guidance and strength, and giving thanks to God for this new opportunity. My papa, my siblings, my mama—they all felt the gravity of what had just happened. They understood, as I did, that this visa meant more than a chance to study.

But the joy was mixed with the bittersweet reality of the visa terms. This visa allowed me one year in the US, renewable as long as I stayed enrolled, but there would be no trips home. We all knew that taking the risk of returning to Haiti at the end of each year could mean the loss of my chance entirely, as there was no guarantee of another visa. I would not see my family again for six, maybe seven years.

As we embraced, they reassured me through tears, "We will miss you terribly, but you are our hope. You are the one God has chosen to break this cycle for us. Go, make a new life. When we see you next, things will be different." Their faith and love filled me with strength, wrapping around me like armor for the journey ahead.

The week passed too quickly. On August 16, we flew back to the States. I left Haiti carrying my family's dreams, love, and prayers back to Minnesota, ready to build the life we had all envisioned. As the seven of us drove home to Detroit Lakes, the significance of the trip and all that it meant settled over us.

For me, it was bittersweet—joy wrapped in sorrow, hope tangled with loss. As much as I longed for the opportunities and dreams ahead, I was wrestling with the reality that once I left, I would not see my family for years.

At the time, I knew having the entire Lee family visit my home country was special, but it wasn't until years later that I fully grasped the profound impact that trip had on everyone involved. I recently asked them about their memories from the trip and came away tearful. The time in Haiti had truly been a turning point for both our families—a journey into the depths of love, sacrifice, and the complexities of human connection.

For John and Mary, it was a testament to their boundless love and the extraordinary sacrifices they were willing to make for their family. They were especially moved by the graciousness of my family, who were obviously so poor, yet so gracious and welcoming. It was so clear that our families cared deeply about each other and respected each other. My family could finally see for themselves how healthy and happy the girls were and that John and Mary would continue to do the best they could for them.

For Carl and Dan, it was an exposure to a way of life so unfamiliar, so far removed from their own, that it was almost impossible to fathom. Carl later shared how seeing how the people carve out their lives from all sorts of seemingly impossible situations really made him appreciate even more what he had back home—and the things people so often take for granted. He said to me, "Coming from somewhere that has so much and going to someplace where people have so much less and yet are still incredibly welcoming and willing to share what they do have with you—I still think about that all the time."

Later Dan told me, "I came to understand the profound privilege of being hosted as we had been. This was more than just providing the outward symbols of hospitality. In a place like Haiti, a country ravaged by colonizers and torn down by dictators, distrust of outsiders would be a reasonable thing to expect. So to be truly welcomed as we were, to be brought in by local people living their lives, created the unique opportunity for deep learning and true human connection. It also gave us a glimpse into the lives of a family who were not objects of pity, but authors of their own development."

For my mama and papa, it was the impossible made possible. Afterward, Mary recalled a moment with my papa. She said, "I will always remember your dad's words as we sat in that circle outside. He said, 'Now that I have seen the girls—how strong and healthy they are—now I can die in peace.'" His words echoed the story of Simeon in the temple (Luke 2:28 32). Farah and Cherline's presence strengthened my father, lifting the heavy cloud of sorrow that had rested on him for over a decade in their absence. That trip was more than a reunion—it was a moment of healing, a restoration of hope, and a testament to the enduring power of family.

For Farah and Cherline, the trip transcended their expectations, filling a void they didn't know was there. It was a journey toward wholeness, a step into embracing every part of themselves. Farah said, "The trip ignited a new side in me. A proud side that no longer wondered where my traits and mannerisms came up. Haiti welcomed us home, and you created a space that felt safe for everyone to rejoice in." Farah and Cherline finally realized that they had come from a loving family that continued to pray for them every day.

Each of us carried something different from this experience in Haiti. Our bond was not just strengthened—it was transformed in ways I never dreamed possible.

Thinking back on this trip, my heart swells with gratitude. Their words are like honey, sweet and sacred, sealing a love and connection that will forever be imprinted on my soul.

CHAPTER 18

Welcome to the Next Six Years

RETURNING TO MINNESOTA felt lighter—I carried a renewed sense of confidence.

That confidence didn't come easily though. I proved to myself that I knew enough English to understand my fast-talking host brother, Carl. I had earned As and Bs in my first year as a junior at the Detroit Lakes High School, despite my limited English. And most importantly, I had received yet another miracle—the opportunity to return and complete my education.

It wasn't just about finishing high school; it was about the possibility of attending a four-year college to study nursing. I was over the moon.

With the F-1 visa now secured in my hands, I knew that this was the start of something entirely new, a rare second chance I couldn't afford to waste. I returned to Detroit Lakes, packed my belongings, and felt the reality of this next step settle in. I would be moving to Moorhead, Minnesota, to begin studying at Oak Grove Lutheran School, a private institution offering faith-based education located in Fargo, North Dakota. Established in 1906, the school has a longstanding history of integrating academics, faith, and service into its curriculum, and I hoped it would be a good fit for me. Each item I packed felt significant, as if my old life and new life were merging into one.

John and Oak Grove had arranged for me to live with Pastor Anne Hokenstad, a teacher from the school who taught religion. It was the perfect setup—each morning, we would ride to school together, sharing quiet conversations that felt grounding. I couldn't have asked for a more comforting presence than Ms. Hokenstad.

Her cozy two-bedroom home on the south side of Moorhead, just a ten-minute drive from campus, was filled with little touches of warmth and familiarity. From the moment I walked through her door, she welcomed me with such kindness, showing me my room and telling me, "This is your space. Make yourself at home." I felt something settle in me, a quiet reassurance. This wasn't just a house—it was a home, one that represented a safe harbor in this new chapter.

My first night in Ms. Hokenstad's home was a quiet one. Sitting on the bed, I looked around the room that now held so much meaning. I whispered a prayer of thanks, filled with hope and gratitude, understanding that this new opportunity was another beautiful gift—a chance to rise beyond the circumstances I'd known and build a life where I could thrive.

As I settled into Oak Grove, I did my best to adapt to the new environment. The academics were intense, much harder without John and Mary by my side as tutors. Ms. Hokenstad helped when she could, but I tried not to lean on her too much. Every teacher at Oak Grove was dedicated and encouraging, making me feel like I could tackle the challenges, even when they felt insurmountable.

In English class that year, I faced an overwhelming challenge: a twelve-page paper. The thought alone terrified me—how could I possibly write twelve pages in English? But the teachers believed in me, and with their guidance, I surprised myself, discovering a resilience I didn't know I had.

Despite the deep sense of belonging I had found, the ache for home never fully left me. Then, something miraculous happened—I discovered there was a Haitian community right in the Fargo-Moorhead area, complete with a Haitian church: Tri-City Haitian Ministry. The news felt like a balm to my homesick heart, and I wasted no time visiting. That's where I met Marie, a young Haitian woman around my age who would come to mean everything to me. We didn't attend the same school, but she lived in the Fargo-Moorhead area with her family and had been there for over a decade. She knew the rhythms, the people, and every nuance of the community. More importantly, she understood me.

Marie became my guide, taking me under her wing and showing me around the city. One of our first stops was her family's home in Fargo. When I entered, I was engulfed in the warmth of Haitian hospitality. Her parents welcomed me like one of their own, with her mother pulling me into a tight embrace, and her father greeting me with a warm smile that seemed to say, "You're safe here." Marie's big brother, WM, was also a quiet source of strength. He was kind and always looked out for me, as a big brother would. His presence made me feel safe and cared for in a world that often felt unfamiliar.

Their family home was filled with the rich, familiar smells of Haitian food, and every meal we shared felt like a taste of home. Sitting around their table, speaking Creole, and laughing over memories of Haiti, I felt like I was back with my own family. The love and acceptance they showed me helped fill the empty spaces that homesickness had carved into my heart.

Marie became my sister, my confidante, and my source of strength. She helped me navigate the hardest days at Oak Grove and cheered me on when my studies felt too heavy. She reminded me why I was here and urged me to keep pushing forward. Her unwavering belief in me lifted me, even in moments when I questioned myself. She would say, "This is just one step. You've come so far, and you're going even further. Don't stop now." Her words filled the silence of my fears with courage.

Before I met Marie, there were many days when I felt deeply lonely—craving the connection of fellow Haitians who understood my culture, my language, and my unspoken grief. That kind of loneliness sat quietly beneath the surface, even in the midst of kindness. Meeting Marie changed that. She saw me, understood me, and brought me a sense of home I didn't realize I was missing. Between the support of Ms. Hokenstad and the Lee family, the care of my teachers, and the loyal friendship of Marie, I found myself embraced by a new kind of family.

Together, they wrapped me in a warmth that softened the hardest days and reminded me that this dream I was chasing wasn't just for me—it was for everyone who had ever believed in me. I was not alone in this new environment. I was part of a community, carried forward by hands that held me up when I needed it most.

All of this hard work, the long nights, and the endless studying— it was leading somewhere, to something extraordinary. With my eyes fixed firmly on college, I felt the door opening wider, paving the way for some of the best news of my life.

COLLEGE

Back in Haiti, my odds of attending college were razor-thin. According to the UNESCO Institute for Statistics: Fewer than 1 percent of Haitians ever attend university[3]—a statistic that loomed over every dream I dared to voice. For most students in my community, finishing high school was the finish line. College was a distant hope, reserved for the elite or for those fortunate enough to have family living abroad who could help.

---

[3] Vital, Louise M. "Higher Education and Career Development Experiences of Emerging Adults: A Focus on University Students and Graduates in Haiti." *African Journal of Career Development.* Accessed August 21, 2025. https:// ajcd.africa/index.php/ajcd/article/view/30/118.

That reality stood in sharp contrast to what I witnessed in Minnesota. American teens treated college as a given. They flipped through brochures, toured campuses, and talked about majors and meal plans like it was all part of a plan they were born into. For them, college was expected. For me, it was a miracle I was chasing with everything I had.

John and Mary encouraged me to consider Concordia College in Moorhead—John's alma mater and the school where their son, Dan, had also graduated. The college was renowned for its rigorous academic programs and exceptional nursing curriculum, aligning perfectly with my aspirations of becoming a nurse. The Lees' stories painted Concordia as a place where I could grow academically, spiritually, and personally, and soon, I began to picture myself there.

At the time, I didn't fully understand the depth of Concordia College's mission: "to influence the affairs of the world by sending into society thoughtful and informed men and women dedicated to the Christian life." But something about those words stirred something in me—even then.

I was pursuing a degree, but I was also searching for purpose. I wanted to be thoughtful and informed. I wanted to serve, to give back, and to use my story to make a difference. Though I didn't yet know the path I would walk, that mission aligned with the cry in my heart—the calling I felt to rise above my circumstances, to lead with faith, and to be a voice for those who didn't have one.

Concordia College, like many other institutions, required international students to take the Test of English as a Foreign Language (TOEFL). This exam would determine whether I could even apply to a US college. Although I had been in the US for nearly two years, I was still learning the language—one phrase, one sentence, one page at a time. John and Mary consistently worked with me to prepare for the exam, especially on weekends when I would travel from Oak Grove to their home—nearly fifty miles away. Those weekends became sacred.

I remember sitting on their porch on freezing winter evenings as I whispered vocabulary words into the cold air, stuffed grammar notes into my coat pockets, and turned every moment into an opportunity to prepare. Each word I learned felt like a defiant whisper back to the silence poverty had tried to impose on me. With flashcards spread across the kitchen table and encouragement in every correction, they helped me push through doubt and fatigue to get one step closer to my dream.

I took the TOEFL exam in early spring of my senior year at Oak Grove. It was trickier than I had anticipated. I struggled through sections that felt like a maze of unfamiliar phrases and subtle differences in meaning. I wasn't confident in my performance—and it showed.

When the results arrived, my heart sank. My score was below Concordia's requirement. I felt like a failure. I had worked so hard—pouring hours into studying tricky word pairs like "further" and "farther," "weather" and "whether," "to," "too," and "two"—words that seemed designed to trip up someone like me. I had believed that hard work would be enough. But in that moment, it didn't feel like it was.

Determined not to give up, I studied even harder and took the test again a month later. This time, I scored well above what Concordia required for international students. With my improved score, I submitted my application to Concordia and prayed.

Every day, I waited anxiously, hoping to hear something that would change the course of my life. I kept replaying thoughts of what life could be like on that campus—immersing myself in studies, meeting new people, and building a future.

Then, on April 9, 2002, it finally arrived—the letter I had dreamed of, prayed over, and waited for with every fiber of my being. Alone in the quiet of my room at Ms. Hokenstad's home, my hands trembled as I opened the envelope. I didn't know whether it held the hope I had dared to believe in—or yet another closed door. I carefully peeled back the seal, the paper trembling between my fingers, and there it was—two words that changed my life forever: "Congratulations, Miquette!"

I clutched the letter, barely able to breathe, and read on through tear-blurred eyes: "The Admission Committee has reviewed your application and is extremely pleased to inform you that you have been accepted for admission to Concordia College. You may begin your studies in the first semester of the 2002–2003 academic year."

My heart surged with emotion. I had done it. Every obstacle, every long night, every tear-filled prayer had led me to this moment. A wave of joy crashed over me.

I called John and Mary immediately. As soon as they answered, I burst into joyful sobs. They were thrilled—celebrating not just my acceptance but all that it represented.

This was liberation, a future beyond anything I had known. It was a victory. It was the key to a life not bound by poverty or limitations but instead defined by endless possibilities. I saw my dreams coming true—a future where I could become who I was meant to be, not just for myself, but for my family and all those who had believed in me. This was the miracle we had prayed for.

I felt a rush of deep gratitude, thinking of everyone who had helped me come this far. Tears filled my eyes as I thought about the family and friends who had lifted me, the mentors who had guided me, and the moments of struggle that had quietly prepared me for this day. Memories of my childhood came flooding back—the dusty roads of St. Michel, the nights without electricity, the dreams I dared to whisper in the dark. I thought of all the things I had once hoped to become, and everything I had fought to overcome.

I knew this acceptance was a breakthrough that would ripple through my family, my community, and everyone who had ever invested in my journey. And a seed of hope was planted in ground that once felt barren.

CHAPTER 19

One Step Closer

WITH MY ACCEPTANCE came the next big question. How was I going to pay for it. The Lees had always planned carefully for their children's education. They were committed to covering their children's undergraduate expenses, giving them a head start in their professional lives without the burden of college debt. This decision reflected their deep belief in the importance of education as a foundation for success.

Their plan was working seamlessly—until I came into the picture.

They had not planned financially for five children to be in college at the same time. This unexpected situation forced John and Mary to re-evaluate their financial priorities. They searched for a way to honor their commitment to education—for their four children and now for me. They had to strategize: How could they help make my dream of becoming a nurse come true while still supporting their own children through college? How could they possibly afford four years at Concordia College for someone who wasn't even born into their family?

After much thought and prayer, they made an unthinkably generous decision: They chose to sell a plot of land that had been in their family for years—land that held deep sentimental value—to create an endowment for my education. When they told me, I was speechless. Overwhelmed. Humbled beyond words.

They didn't just make room for me in their home. They made a permanent place for me in their hearts—and in their future. The reality of that sacrifice settled into my soul. Their faith in me, their willingness to give up something so treasured, became a responsibility I carried with deep reverence. I was determined to make their sacrifice count.

On May 25, 2002, at twenty-one years old, I walked across the stage at Oak Grove Lutheran School wearing a burgundy cap and gown, shoulder to shoulder with thirty-six other graduating seniors. Everyone was excited that day, but for me, this moment carried a significance far beyond a simple ceremony. I was the first in my family to take that step—to officially complete high school.

For my parents back in Haiti, it meant they could finally check off something they had long prayed for: They had a child who completed school. I carried that honor with pride—for every sacrifice, every prayer, every ounce of hope they had poured into my future.

To celebrate, I shared a graduation party in the school cafeteria with another international student from Japan. We invited friends, classmates, and of course, John and Mary, who had walked this journey with me every step of the way. Farah and Cherline were there, too—beaming with pride. The joy in that room was unforgettable. It was an amazing chapter coming to a close, while another exciting one was just beginning.

That summer, I volunteered at Concordia Language Villages at Lac du Bois, where I immersed myself in the energy and diversity of language and culture. Then I spent time helping with summer Bible camp at John's parish—an experience I absolutely loved. Those moments of service, connection, and growth deepened my faith and reminded me that I wasn't just preparing for college—I was preparing for life.

I also poured myself into studying for my driver's education lessons. John and Mary believed strongly in independence, and they saw driving as an essential part of that (even after my disastrous first lesson with John). They wanted me to have the freedom to navigate life confidently on my own.

The first time I took my driving test, I failed because of the parallel parking portion. That mistake made me incredibly anxious for my second attempt.

Determined that I must pass, John and Mary practiced with me countless times, especially focusing on what had caused me to fail in the first place. They were patient, and I was grateful for their support. A month later, I was back at the DMV. I felt confident and ready. I got behind the wheel and followed the instructor's directions with ease.

Everything was going smoothly until we approached an intersection with a blind stop—one of those where you have to inch forward past the stop sign to actually see the oncoming traffic. Thinking I was being a good, rule-following student, I stopped right at the sign and then drove away.

Back at the DMV parking lot, the instructor looked at me and said, "You did a great job, but I can't pass you. You didn't creep forward past the blind intersection before proceeding."

My heart sank. Not again. I needed this license before heading to work at Valleyfair, an amusement park in Shakopee, Minnesota. Time wasn't on my side.

When the instructor shattered my dream with, "I cannot pass you," I instinctively hit my forehead on the steering wheel with a loud thud and blurted out, "No, no, no! You can't fail me! I promise I'll creep at every blind intersection from now on. I'll be a great driver. Please, don't fail me!"

To my surprise, the instructor chuckled and said, "You don't have to cry. I'm not passing you because you're upset, but … I believe in you."

And just like that—I PASSED! Whoo-hoo!

In just a few short months, I would be heading to Concordia. However, financially, there was still a long way to go. John invited me to attend the summer Synod Clergy Conference in Detroit Lakes. During the conference, he shared with other attendees my desire to attend Concordia and the financial challenges I faced. In that room full of strangers, something incredible happened—a hat was passed around, and many of the attendees donated toward my education.

I will never forget the many hands that came together to make my dream a reality—it truly took a village. That moment was a powerful reminder that I was not alone. It showed me the kindness and generosity of people who believed in my future, even when they had just met me. Their willingness to give reinforced what I already knew deep in my heart: Education changes lives, and when people come together to support a dream, anything is possible.

STEP FORWARD IF

It was a beautiful August day when John, Mary, Farah, and Cherline made the 45-mile drive from Detroit Lakes to Concordia with me. As we carried my belongings up to Hoyum Hall third floor, I was overwhelmed by a swirl of awe, disbelief, and deep gratitude. This was the day I had longed for—the one I had whispered about in quiet prayers under Haitian skies. And now, it was real. I was about to start college. No longer on the outside looking in. No more wondering if a future like this could ever be mine. It was unfolding right before me.

True to their generous nature, John and Mary did for me what they had done for their sons, Dan and Carl. They opened a checking account in my name and arranged a monthly allowance—carefully planned to meet my personal needs and cover school expenses. It wasn't just financial support—it was another layer of trust, of belief in my potential.

Once everything was unpacked, John and Mary offered parting words—soft, sincere, and full of love. They encouraged me to manage my time wisely, to stay focused, and to always remember the dreams that had brought me this far. Their goodbye was tender but weighty, as though they were entrusting me with something sacred. I listened intently, storing every word like treasure. I knew their wisdom would become my compass in the unknown days ahead.

After they left, a heavy silence settled in. I leaned against the glass window of my third-floor room, staring out at a world that felt both familiar and foreign. The room itself, though small, suddenly felt enormous—echoing with possibility and the ache of transition. The air hung thick with emotion, the kind that rises in your chest when your life is quietly but undeniably shifting.

As I stood there, my mind traveled back to St. Michel. I saw a little girl with big, impossible dreams of becoming a nurse—a little girl who dared to hope despite the reality pressing down on her. She dreamed boldly, but behind that boldness was fear. Fear of dreaming too big. Fear of wanting too much in a world where her family's circumstances seemed determined to keep her small.

And yet, here I was.

I fixed up my bunk bed with fresh bedding the Lees had bought just for the occasion—the lower bunk was mine—and looked up at the top bunk where my roommate, a young woman, Enetty from Zimbabwe, would soon sleep. I was overwhelmed. I had dreamed about this, but the reality was so much more than I could have ever imagined. I was here, in a dorm room, preparing for college classes. Every breath felt like it was filling my lungs with the magnitude of this incredible new beginning.

Monday morning came, and I walked to the bookstore, ready to buy my textbooks. When I saw the prices, I could barely process it—spending that much on books alone felt almost unthinkable. I hesitated but reminded myself that these books represented knowledge and growth. This was my chance to learn and rise above everything that had held me back. I took a deep breath and bought them, each book a symbol of my commitment to this journey.

Orientation day was just as surreal. Among the many new faces and traditions, one stood out: the iconic "Cobber Beanie." This bright yellow hat, handed to every new freshman, was a rite of passage, symbolizing our official entry into the Concordia community.

At first glance, I thought the beanie looked a little ridiculous. But as I held it in my hands, I began to understand its significance. It wasn't just a hat—it was a symbol of belonging, a tangible reminder that I was now part of something bigger. With a mix of pride and humility, I placed it on my head.

During orientation, as I looked around and saw hundreds of new students wearing the same bright yellow beanie, I felt an unexpected sense of unity. We were all starting fresh, stepping into this shared journey together. For most of my life, I had felt like an outsider. But here, I was welcomed—not just by the college but by a new community that would be my home.

One activity during orientation will stay with me forever. It was called "Step Forward If." The leader asked us a series of questions, and we were to step forward if the statement applied to us.

In retrospect, I believe the leader chose this icebreaker to foster connection, assuming that most students who could afford to attend Concordia had some degree of financial stability—especially international students. I'm sure the activity wasn't meant to single anyone out or leave anyone behind. But my situation had always been different from most.

It went like this:

"Step forward if you lived with both parents." As a child, I did, so I proudly stepped forward.

"Step forward if you come from a large family." I smiled and stepped forward again.

"Step forward if you have traveled to a different country." I came from Haiti ... my proudest step!

With each step, I felt a rush of exhilaration. But those were the only few steps I would take, as the questions soon became more sophisticated:

- Step forward if you are an only child.

- Step forward if you ever had a birthday party.

- Step forward if your parents took a vacation with you.

- Step forward if you had electricity in your home.

- Step forward if you had a refrigerator.

- Step forward if you had a TV in your home.

- Step forward if your parents had graduated high school.

As I watched my classmates step forward with each question—even the more complex ones, like "Step forward if your parents had college or PhD degrees."—I realized just how far I was from the economic ladder at my new school.

I had always known I came from poverty, that my life was different from many others here. But this activity lay it bare in a way I had never felt before. As I stood there, watching my peers move forward again and again, I felt the burden of my story—my past, my family, the sacrifices, the pain.

But instead of shrinking, something powerful rose within me. This moment, this experience, became a turning point. I was more determined than ever to make the most of every opportunity and create a future that would honor everything I had endured to stand in that line.

Orientation week was an emotional whirlwind. I met students from places I'd only read about and bonded with other international students over our shared experience of being far from home. Osaki, Lynn, Sylvester, Jackie, and Ruth quickly became close friends. Together, we navigated unfamiliar territory, finding a sense of belonging in each other's company.

The International Organization of Students (IOS) also became a source of comfort. The IOS lounge was my refuge—a space where I connected with others who understood the homesickness, fear, and excitement without needing words. They became my family, my lifeline, filling the emptiness of being so far from home.

Settling into life at Concordia wasn't easy, but it was beautiful. I studied harder than I ever had before, pushing myself through every challenge that came my way. Every class, every assignment, every late night in the library felt like a step toward a better future.

Still, I have to admit, it was overwhelming at times. The pressure felt immense. I wasn't just doing all this for myself. I was doing it for an entire family. For my parents who never got the chance. For my siblings who dreamed they could have had that opportunity. For every child in Haiti who dreamed without knowing whether dreams could come true. The weight pushed me forward and urged me on, but it also wore on me. I often felt the responsibility of it all pressing on my shoulders.

But here I was, in America, holding my dream in my hands, and I couldn't let it slip away.

At Concordia, my advisor helped me choose my first classes, including biology and chemistry. But while I could navigate biology, chemistry was a mountain I felt I'd never climb. I tried everything—flashcards, late-night study sessions, countless notes. But every time I thought I understood, something new would knock me down. I remember sitting in that lecture hall, watching my classmates nod along, wondering why it seemed so easy for them. When the semester ended, I barely passed with a D. I held back tears of relief, grateful I wouldn't have to repeat it, but I also felt a wave of doubt. This one class had nearly shattered my confidence—could I really do this?

In the spring of 2003, it was time to apply to the nursing program, and that all-too-familiar fear resurfaced. I had completed my freshman year and assumed that admission into the nursing program would be a natural next step—without the need for an application. To my surprise, it wasn't. Students from the college still had to apply, and I learned that only a select few were chosen each year from an overwhelming number of applications. Hearing this news was devastating.

There were so many applicants—each with their own story, each fighting for one of the limited spots. *How could I possibly stand out?* My grades were not exceptional, but I knew I had something else to offer: resilience, an unrelenting drive to turn my dream into reality, and a purpose greater than myself. My ambition was rooted in the hope of changing lives, especially those back home in Haiti.

Part of the application process included writing an essay—a chance to make your case. *Why should we choose you?* That was the question.

I poured my heart into my essay. I chose to write about my childhood in Haiti and how nursing had always been my beacon, my purpose. I shared the painful truth about losing two of my siblings to preventable illnesses due to lack of healthcare—a loss that shaped my resolve to make a difference.

I explained that this dream wasn't just mine—it was the hope of everyone who had believed in me and lifted me out of poverty. I described my community, where nurses were revered as heroes, and how I longed to be one of them—to bring healing and hope to those who needed it most. I wrote about my family, who believed in my dream and whose faith in me kept me going, even when the odds seemed insurmountable.

As I handed in my essay, my hands trembled—not from fear of rejection but from the significance of everything this essay represented. I knew my chances were slim.

The nursing department sent out letters in June, determining the fate of prospective students. The wait felt endless. My mind raced through backup plans, but none felt right.

And then—I got the letter. I had been accepted.

I couldn't believe it. I had been chosen. My heart swelled, and a fire ignited within me. I was one step closer!

CHAPTER 20

Not Finished Yet

I ENROLLED IN the nursing program in the spring of my sopho-more year, and it was even harder than I'd expected. Every test, every assignment felt like a make-or-break moment. Each class carried its own weight, leaving no room for error. I stayed up late, working through complex concepts, translating unfamil-iar vocabulary, and fighting through exhaustion. I wanted to excel—I wanted to prove to myself and to everyone who believed that I was capable.

But it was overwhelming. Writing papers, which came easily to my classmates, took me hours. The Reading and Writing Center became my refuge. The tutors there, with their patient smiles and encouraging words, helped me put my thoughts on paper when the English words felt just out of reach. They were my sup-port—my quiet cheerleaders—through long nights of study and moments of self-doubt.

Despite all my efforts, I still felt like I was barely keeping up.

I had to make some major changes. Before attending Concordia, I longed to be in the choir under Dr. René Clausen, an American composer, conductor, and three-time Grammy Award–winning choir director. I had watched my host brother, Dan, flourish in the choir under his leadership, and I aspired to join as well.

The Concordia choir was almost like a full major with the level of commitment required. Since the women's choir had a lighter commitment, I decided to audition for it. After my audition, I was thrilled to receive a call—I had made the cut! I was overjoyed and honored to have the privilege of performing in the grand Christmas concert, a truly magical experience set against Concordia's breathtaking murals.

I loved my time in the choir. It was where I felt the freest, especially after long hours of classes. Each practice became a sanctuary, a space where music allowed me to escape my worries and simply be present. I cherished every moment—the harmonies, the camaraderie, the sheer joy of singing.

But as my nursing studies became more demanding, I faced a difficult choice. The rigor of my coursework left little room for rehearsals and performances, and I knew I had to make a sacrifice. With a heavy heart, I said goodbye to singing in the choir, trading it for my calling—one that required my full dedication.

In the fall of 2005, with two semesters left in the nursing program, I found myself contemplating a significant change: switching my major. Nursing had been my dream for as long as I could remember, an aspiration tied to my childhood. It was a career that held dignity and purpose, and I had wanted that life of service. Yet, here I was, grappling with chemistry exams, late nights, and a nagging sense that perhaps my strengths lay elsewhere.

It took me days to craft the perfect message to tell my guardians, John and Mary, about my decision to switch majors. When I finally mustered the courage, I hit send at 10:30 p.m., unsure of what their reaction would be. To my surprise, their response was swift—they drove to Moorhead the very next day for a heart-to-heart talk at my 8th Avenue French dormitory. Seeing them at my doorstep made me realize just how serious this was.

Their compassion and discernment were evident from the start. They didn't lecture or impose their opinions; instead, they asked thoughtful, specific questions, wanting to understand why. They listened intently as I explained the overwhelming pressure and my fears of failing. With quiet strength, they reminded me of my childhood dream of becoming a nurse—a dream that once seemed impossible growing up in Haiti.

Their words weren't forceful but filled with encouragement. They pointed out how healthcare transcends borders and how nursing could be a gateway not just to a degree but to a life of impact. They reminded me of the little girl who once dreamed of being a community nurse, the child who believed she could bring hope and healing to others.

After that conversation, I paused, prayed, and searched for clarity. John and Mary's compassionate intervention gave me the perspective I needed. Their belief in me reignited something I had forgotten: the resilience that had brought me this far. I re-strategized and threw myself back into clinicals, despite the grueling hours and sleepless nights. I reminded myself of the privilege of being in one of the most beautiful campuses in the US, learning from brilliant minds, and pursuing a dream I thought would never happen.

After speaking with John and Mary, I felt a surge of energy.

Nursing wasn't just a challenge—it was a calling, a path that would shape me and allow me to make a difference in the lives of others. And I'm so glad I stuck with it.

With their encouragement and the steadfast support of my advisors, Jean Bokinskie and Polly Kloster, I pushed through the toughest moments. Dr. Jack Rydell, who taught two of my classes, was also especially helpful. They dedicated their time to help me grasp difficult concepts, and their faith in my ability carried me forward.

By my senior year, clinical rotations became our primary focus as nursing students, especially in the final semester. During this time, I realized that I was naturally skilled at hands-on patient care. My preceptors and the nurses I worked with at the hospital often complimented me on my abilities, and my advisor, Polly, was pleased to receive such positive feedback about her student.

Hearing those encouraging words filled me with gratitude for John and Mary—their unwavering belief in me made all the difference. They knew I could do the work, and because of them, I believed it, too.

Switching majors wasn't the answer—resilience was. It was all part of the journey that shaped me into who I am today. And when I finally submitted my last paper, I knew it had all been worth it.

The eve of my college graduation was nothing short of spectacular. As was my custom before every big event in my life, I could barely sleep. I lay in bed and reflected on the journey that had brought me here and how the next day would redefine everything. For generations, no one in my family had graduated from high school, let alone college. Tomorrow, the narrative of my family would change. No longer would anyone say that no one in our family had ever gone to college. I was the first to reach this pinnacle, and being the one to forge this new legacy felt both humbling and exhilarating. Tomorrow, I would carry the pride of this achievement not just for myself but for everyone who had dreamed of this moment. Tomorrow, everything would be different.

Waking up the next morning, I was filled with an indescribable excitement. April 30, 2006 had arrived—the day I had dreamed of.

Friends traveled from far and wide to witness the moment. Among the audience was Mommy Carme, along with her son, Ruby, and nephew Yveto, who made the long drive from Chicago to be there for this monumental milestone. My Haitian community showed up in full support, their cheers filling the room and lifting my heart.

As I put on my gown, a surge of overwhelming gratitude washed over me for everyone who had made this day possible, for the sacrifices they had made. When my name was called, I walked onto that stage with immense pride, representing my mama, papa, and siblings who never had this chance. I walked tall, my chest puffed up, my head held high, as I accepted my diploma and shook hands with President Pamela Jolicoeur. I was on cloud nine.

The journey had been long and grueling, filled with moments of doubt and quiet battles no one else could see. But at that moment, it was real—I had crossed the finish line. Joy filled me, warm and buoyant, as if every struggle had finally been worth it.

But something shifted deep inside me during the ceremony. Reverend Dr. Donald Messer, the commencement speaker, stepped forward and raised his hand. *Snap. Snap. Snap.* The sharp sound of his fingers echoed through the hall.

"Every three seconds," he said, his voice heavy with meaning. "Someone, somewhere, dies from a lack of water, healthcare, or education."

The room fell silent, but in my mind, his snaps kept echoing. *Snap. Snap. Snap.* Three seconds. Another life gone. Three more seconds. Gone again.

My thoughts shifted to my family in Haiti. Faces flashed in my mind—my parents, my siblings, my community. I thought of my two siblings who had died from poverty, their absence still an open wound in my heart. They weren't just numbers in a statistic. They had names, dreams, and lives that should have been lived. The ache of it swelled in my chest, raw and unrelenting.

Suddenly, my finish line didn't feel like the end of the race.

I've always admired those who dedicate their lives to service— people who pour themselves into something greater than their own comfort or success. Hearing that speech made my resolve even stronger.

As I sat there, my thoughts drifted to Concordia's mission: "to influence the affairs of the world by sending into society thoughtful and informed men and women dedicated to the Christian life." What a powerful call to action. And it echoed something I had heard long before—Rotary's motto: "Service Above Self."

Together, those two ideals began to reshape how I saw my future. Those words engraved themselves into my mind. They gave language to what I already believed: Education is not an end in itself but a beginning. A foundation for service. A tool for justice. A way to live out the gospel with courage and conviction.

That day, something clicked. My journey wasn't about achieving personal success or even lifting up my family—it was about something much bigger. It was about service. It was about influence. It was about impact.

My vision became clear: I wanted to generate lasting change in Haiti through education. I wanted to be part of the solution, to create opportunities where there had been none, and to help other children like me dream beyond survival. That speech didn't just inspire me—it *commissioned* me. I left more determined than ever to live out both Concordia's mission and Rotary's call and to dedicate my life to service that would outlive me.

This is it, Miquette—you are a college graduate, but the work is not yet finished.

I was the first in my family to graduate college, holding a bachelor's degree in nursing. But this was only the beginning. The world wasn't done with me yet.

GETTING BACK UP AGAIN

After graduation, I stepped into a new job as a graduate nurse at St. Mary's Hospital in Detroit Lakes, while preparing for the NCLEX exam scheduled for the first week of June. Once again, everything depended on a test.

But even amid the pressure, stepping into the hospital as a nurse for the first time felt like I was living someone else's life. I was so close. Seeing my badge with the title Graduate Nurse printed on it was awesome—like holding a piece of my dream in my hands. Putting on my scrubs and caring for patients filled me with a deep sense of purpose. It was hard work—but it was sacred work. And I loved every minute of it.

On the day of the exam, John drove me the four hours to Brooklyn Park. As we neared the building where the exam was being held, my heart felt like it was pounding out of my chest. I knew the stakes—passing this test meant I could finally become a registered nurse, and the idea of failure felt too devastating to even imagine.

I sat at the computer inside of a small cubical, every fiber of my being tense. I started answering the questions, and each one felt like a mountain. They were so much harder than I'd expected, with calculations and chemistry problems that clawed at my confidence. After 170 questions, the test abruptly ended. That was it. It was over. Now came the waiting, with everything I had fought for hanging in the balance.

Weeks passed before I got the alert that my score was available. My hands shook as I logged in, my heart pounding with dread.

FAILED.

The word stared back at me—FAILED—cold and final. I felt my heart shatter, the ground slipping beneath me. Tears poured down my face. I had come so far, over-come so much, only to be stopped at the very edge of my dream. The pain was overwhelming.

John and Mary tried to comfort me, assuring me that I would pass next time. But I felt lost—completely disoriented. I couldn't eat. I couldn't sleep. I walked around the house in a daze, replay-ing the test in my mind, wondering where I had gone wrong. To others, I probably looked like a shell of myself—quiet, with-drawn, unable to find words for the burden I was carrying. It wasn't just the test I had failed—it felt like I had let everyone down: my family, my mentors, my country.

After failing the NCLEX, the hospital had to follow protocol and terminate my position as a graduate nurse until I passed. It was a crushing blow. Working at a US hospital as an RN before returning to Haiti had been crucial—not just to gain experience but to earn an income that would allow me to invest in Haiti and support my family, who was relying on me. The job at St. Mary's I'd worked so hard to start was suddenly gone. Failing meant I couldn't practice—not until I passed. Everything felt like it was slipping away.

I began to question everything: *Am I good enough? Am I smart enough? Was it foolish to believe I could achieve this dream?* I had heard stories of nursing graduates who took the NCLEX count-less times without passing. I began to wonder if I would become one of them.

Then a light appeared—Mommy Carme. After learning about my test result, she invited me to stay with her for a week in Chicago to help ease my disappointment. John and Mary, who felt my pain, encouraged me as well, assuring me that a change of scenery might be just what I needed to recharge.

I accepted her invitation and found refuge in her home, where she cared for me with the gentleness and love of a mother. She nourished my spirit, held space for my pain, and reminded me of my worth. She nursed me back to life.

After a week in Chicago, I returned to Minnesota with renewed determination. I buried myself in study books, resolved to take the NCLEX a second—and final—time. Too many people, especially the Lees, had sacrificed, supported, and believed in me for me to give up now.

I pushed myself harder than ever, praying that God would grant me the courage and calm I needed to overcome my fear. I scheduled my retake for July 7, 2006, and made the four-hour drive once more. Every mile of that trip felt like a heartbeat, my entire story flashing before my eyes.

I prayed one last time as I sat down at the computer, asking God for peace—no matter the outcome. As the test began, I felt a surprising calm settle over me. I started answering the questions, more focused and confident than I had been during my first attempt. Then, after just 70 questions—compared to the 170 I had taken the first time—the test ended.

I froze for a moment, my heart pounding. I took a deep breath, unsure what it meant, but holding onto one truth: I had done all I could.

The wait that followed was pure agony, though I did my best not to let it show. Each day stretched endlessly, each hour thick with uncertainty as I held my breath—knowing my future hung in the balance. But John and Mary could tell. They sensed the anxiety I was trying to mask and did their best to distract me, gently encouraging me to get involved in as many church activities as possible. From helping with Sunday school to volunteering at youth group events, they kept me busy—and grounded.

Then, finally, the alert came: My score was available.

My heart pounded as I logged in, my hands trembling, my breath shallow. And then, there it was ...

"Miquette, an NCLEX examination applicant for the Minnesota Board of Nursing, HAS PASSED the National Council Licensure Examination for Registered Nurses."

I screamed—a cry so deep it seemed to rise from the very depths of my soul. My voice broke with relief, joy, and overwhelming gratitude. I had done it.

After everything—the sacrifices, the doubts, the heartbreak—I was officially an RN. My childhood dream was finally real. I whispered through tears, "*Mèsi Jezi.*" "Thank You, Jesus."

My parents, my grandparents, and all who came before them had lived in the shadow of scarcity. Education had always been out of reach, a distant dream unattainable in a cycle where survival took precedence over hope. But God, in His infinite grace, had intervened. Through the power of education, the generosity of John and Mary and countless others, and the unwavering support of Rotary International, He had opened a door for me.

After seeing the word "PASSED" on the screen, I screamed once more at the top of my lungs: "John! Mary!" I bolted down the stairs like a madwoman, tears already spilling from my eyes. They rushed toward me, startled at first—but when they saw my face, they knew.

We collapsed into each other's arms in the middle of the living room, hugging, crying, laughing all at once. Tears streamed down our cheeks as they held me tightly, whispering, "Congratulations, Miquette! You did it!" This victory belonged to all of us. We had all carried this dream, and now we were standing in its fulfillment.

I wish I could have picked up the phone to call my family in Haiti to share the good news. But they had no phone, no email—no way for me to reach them. All I could do was imagine the joy they would have felt if they had known. I pictured their faces, their pride, the tears that might have matched my own. Even in their silence, I carried them with me in that moment of triumph.

Later, I proudly shared the news with my supervisor at St. Mary's. Their excitement filled me with pride, and not long after, St. Mary's Hospital welcomed me back—this time as a full-fledged registered nurse.

But even in the celebration, my focus quickly shifted to the next goal of helping those back home. Every shift, every patient, every step forward became part of the greater vision I carried: a better future for Haiti, built through education and hope.

I poured myself into my work. I picked up every extra shift I could at the hospital and even took a second job at a nursing home in my neighborhood. My days were long, and the work was demanding, but I had a vision. I wanted to provide for my family, *and* I wanted to equip them to thrive. I now knew that education was the key, the one thing that could truly break the cycle of poverty and give them a voice. My dream had grown. I wanted not just to give them resources but to give them tools, as the common phrase goes: teach them how to fish, not just feed them for a day.

Feeling a deep sense of responsibility, I approached John and Mary and offered to contribute financially now that I was earning a paycheck. For six years, they had supported me in every way, and I wanted to give back. To my surprise, they refused. "We'll continue to care for you just as we always have," they said. They insisted I stay rent-free and encouraged me to save as much as possible, knowing I had only one year to prepare before returning home.

I set my sights on saving every penny, knowing that my return to Haiti was my chance to give back to the people who had carried me here with their prayers, sacrifices, and faith in me.

CHAPTER 21

Homecoming

MELISSA, KNOWN AS "Camisha," was the youngest of my parents' children—the surprise baby. Born on October 23, 1991, her story was very different from the rest of ours. Her adoption had been arranged before she was even born. With the help of the orphanage that Farah and Cherline were adopted through, Gladys facilitated Camisha's adoption process with a family in Canada. Our parents told us that a wonderful home was already waiting for her.

We only had a few days with her before she was gone. Though there wasn't enough time to build a deep bond, her absence left a void nonetheless. I often wondered what it would have been like to grow up with her—to play with her, laugh with her, and see glimpses of ourselves in her smile.

It was heartbreaking for my parents to give up another child to adoption, but poverty left them with no other choice. They did what they had to do—not because they didn't love us, but because they loved us enough to endure lifelong heartache for the hope of a better future. They gave everything they could, including pieces of their own hearts, to give their children a chance at a life beyond survival.

In 2007, Camisha and parents Barb and Roger decided to visit me in Minnesota before I returned to Haiti. I had dreamed of Camisha—the sibling I never had the chance to know. When her adoptive family reached out to say she was coming to visit, I could hardly believe it.

I was elated when I got to do something small for Misha, just as I had done for my other sisters, Cherline and Farah. She let me braid her hair, and oh, how I cherished that tender moment. It was simple, quiet, but deeply intimate—the kind of memory that stays etched in your soul forever. We shared a room during her visit to Detroit Lakes, staying up late to talk and laugh, to fill in the gaps of time lost. Telling her about our biological family—our roots, our shared story—was something I will always treasure. It was a sacred exchange, soul to soul.

Misha later traveled to Haiti on several occasions to meet my parents and the rest of her biological family. Watching her embrace that part of her identity filled me with gratitude and pride. I will always be thankful to her parents, Barb and Roger, for planting and nurturing the love of family in her heart. Even as a little girl, they encouraged her to write letters to our parents whenever missionaries from their church traveled to Haiti. Unlike the letters sent by John and Mary, our family did receive the ones from Misha. Those letters were priceless treasures to us—little lifelines of hope and love in a world where we didn't know if we'd ever meet her.

But we did. And in that meeting, something fractured was made whole.

Her visit only ignited the fire in me to see my family in Haiti all the more. Her presence stirred a longing I couldn't ignore—a deep ache for home, to reconnect and embrace the people who had sacrificed so much for us, and to tell them, face-to-face, that their love had never been forgotten.

In the days leading up to my trip back to Haiti, I often lay in bed, staring at the ceiling, reflecting on how much had changed. Seven years ago, my family's reality was unimaginable to most. We lived in a house with no running water, no indoor plumbing, and sporadic electricity. Proper nutrition was a luxury we couldn't afford. Healthcare was out of reach. We didn't know anything about the lives of my sisters Farah, Cherline, and Camisha. Life was a daily struggle to survive, and the idea of breaking free felt impossible.

But now, as I prepared to step back onto Haitian soil, I carried with me not only resources to help my family but also hope— real, tangible hope. My family still had challenges, but they no longer faced them alone. They knew they could count on me.

As I thought about the transformation, tears filled my eyes. God had done what no one else could.

On June 11, 2007, I returned to Haiti a changed person. The young girl who had left seven years earlier—burdened by hunger, uncertainty, and the fight for survival—was gone. In her place stood a woman who had witnessed God's miracles firsthand, a woman armed with education, faith, and an unshakable determination to make a difference.

I wasn't alone. The person who had facilitated my exit, John, returned with me, and he carried my dreams back home with him. John packed a backpack for himself and used his two suitcases and carry-on allowance for my belongings. I made the most of every inch of the luggage I was allowed—two large suitcases, one carry-on, and a personal bag that was practically a second carry-on. Each bag was filled to the brim with clothes, essentials, and pieces of the new life I was bringing home.

This was my homecoming, and I wasn't coming back empty-handed. I was bringing with me everything I had fought for, everything I had been given, everything I had become.

As I stepped off the plane in Haiti, my chest tightened and my heartbeat quickened. A rush of warmth swept through me, almost as if the very air was embracing me. My knees felt weak beneath me, yet my spirit felt lighter than it had in years. I was home.

This was my victory, but it was also a victory for my parents, who had prayed through every hardship. It was a victory for my siblings, who now had the opportunity to dream beyond survival. It was a testament to the vision of Rotary International, which believed education could change lives.

Above all, it was a reminder of God's faithfulness. The God who had carried me through the storms had now brought me full circle. As I stood on Haitian soil once again, I knew this was only the beginning of what He would do—through all those who would dare to believe that with Him, nothing is impossible.

My heart was full of hope. I believed I was ready—to reintegrate, to serve, to let God use me however He wished. I imagined myself stepping right back into the rhythms of home, equipped with new knowledge and resources to make a difference. But I hadn't anticipated how hard it would be.

Haiti hadn't changed—I had. The streets I once walked barefoot, the poverty I once endured, now struck me as an unbearable burden. Seeing children hungry, barefoot, desperate—things I had once accepted as normal—now brought a pain I couldn't shake. Parents came to me pleading for food, and I often stood silent, heartbroken and overwhelmed.

I realized something I had never seen before: When you live in survival mode, you have no capacity to notice others' pain. Years ago, I hadn't seen the suffering around me—not because I didn't care, but because I simply couldn't. My own hunger, my own struggle consumed every thought. Now, with my basic needs met, I was finally able to see the bigger picture—and it was heartbreaking.

Meanwhile, my family had changed, too—dramatically.

While working in the US, I sent back whatever I could. I convinced my mother to retire from her exhausting job in a group home, promising her a monthly stipend so she could finally rest. Slowly, change took root.

When I came home, I hardly recognized the life I had left. My family now had solid homes with electricity, plumbing, beds to sleep in, and multiple rooms. Gone were the long days of everyone crowding into one cramped room. The uncertainty and lack of space were replaced by comfort and dignity.

This kind of living gave us a sense of accomplishment. It brought us closer together. There was less bickering now, maybe because we weren't constantly on top of each other anymore. There was a real peace—and something truly beautiful—about the new living arrangement. For the first time, our home didn't just feel like a shelter; it felt like a place to breathe, to rest, to grow.

My own life had changed, too—more than I ever imagined. I got an important job that came with a beautiful home and a full staff. The house I lived in was immaculate—clean, orderly, and nothing like the chaos I once knew. I now lived in a space with multiple rooms, running water, and modern amenities. My kitchen was stocked with three meals a day—and even snacks I didn't need. It was a world away from the one-room house I had grown up in, where food was never guaranteed and "luxury" meant having enough to fill our stomachs. At times, I felt a deep, aching guilt for the comfort I now enjoyed.

But not everyone I loved was living in that peace and privilege. Many of the friends I had left behind were still living a life marked by scarcity, instability, and daily hardship. I had changed, and my circumstances had changed, but theirs had not. It left me feeling disoriented, torn between gratitude and grief.

I struggled to reconcile the two worlds I was living between. *How could I sleep soundly when others slept on dirt floors? How could I enjoy abundance when so many had nothing? How could I celebrate the transformation in my own life while others remained stuck in a cycle I knew all too well?*

The truth is, I never fully adjusted to life in Haiti again. The disparity was too grave, too persistent, too heavy to carry day after day. The comfort I lived in constantly clashed with the suffering I witnessed. My heart stayed restless.

But that restlessness became a constant reminder of why I was there—not to be comfortable but to be faithful.

I wasn't called to fix everything—I was called to *do* something. And that something, through God, could still grow into more than I ever imagined.

CHAPTER 22

Common Ground

IN THE SPRING of 2008, I began my search for a meaningful job in Port-au-Prince. A good friend, Laurie Desir, whom I met through the Lees as result of their mutual adoption circle, had referred me for a substitute teaching role at a local English speaking international Christian school named Quisqueya Christian School (QCS). I filled in a few times that season. With each visit, I felt a growing sense of belonging—it was a place that felt right.

That summer, Laurie shared that the school was looking to hire a full-time nurse, and she believed I was perfect for the position. I scheduled an interview with the headmaster right away.

On the day of the interview, I walked into the office and was greeted by two women who radiated warmth. Mirna and Danie. Mirna, the office manager, welcomed me with a smile that felt like a soothing embrace. It wasn't just polite—it was the kind of smile that said, *Take a deep breath. You've got this.*

When I was offered the school nurse position, I was overjoyed. The role paired my two greatest passions: education and nursing. I couldn't believe I had the chance to care for students while also being part of their learning environment. It felt like a dream come true, a space where I could serve with both skill and heart.

From that moment on, Mirna and Danie, two incredible women, became more than just colleagues—they became my closest friends. We shared laughter, long days, and countless stories. However, the instant Danie learned I was single, her focus shifted. She became a woman on a mission—determined to find me a husband.

I grew up knowing I wanted a better life—one that allowed me to be self-sufficient and uplift my family. By the grace of God, I achieved that milestone. However, while I focused on my work, I also longed to have a family of my own. I had returned to Haiti a year earlier and had a few dating adventures along the way—mostly learning that some relationships serve more as "educational experiences." Danie was determined to write the love story she knew was meant to be.

Danie set her sights on Art, the health and PE teacher at Quisqueya Christian School. She was determined to match us. She orchestrated moments and conversations with the precision of someone who believed love was inevitable. And as it turned out, she was right.

Art was from Ohio. He had first come to Haiti in 2000 for a semester and fell in love with the country. That initial visit planted something deep in his heart—a calling he couldn't shake. So in the spring of 2008, he returned to Haiti to teach at QCS.

I still remember my first impression of Art. His calm and funny demeanor stood out immediately. He carried himself with quiet confidence, but his presence was electric—not in a loud or flashy way but in the warmth and peace he brought into every room. There was something different about him, something steady and grounded.

We often joke about when he first "noticed me." In September of 2008, shortly after he moved to Haiti to teach, a hurricane hit. A mission compound was devastated from the rain and a dam break upriver. Our school organized a service project for students to help with the clean-up. He was the lone chaperone and asked in a teacher meeting if other adults would like to join, so I volunteered. He didn't know my background and had his doubts about how much mud and debris removal I would be willing to perform. He likes to tell this next part: "The morning we were preparing to leave, students came in dirty work clothes and boots ... and then came Miquette. Nice jeans, makeup done, hoop earrings, and something I'm sure she would call 'cute' shoes. But from the moment we arrived, Miquette served with joy! All day long she moved branches, shoveled mud, and encouraged those who had lost much." Art and I had talked before that day, but it was the first time he saw something different in me.

Art was easy to talk to, and our conversations always flowed naturally—about our students, our shared love for Haiti, our lives, and most meaningfully, our faith. What drew me in the most was his fierce love for Jesus. It was evident in how he lived, how he treated others, how he carried himself with humility and conviction. That kind of faith speaks louder than words, and it made a deep impression on me.

At first, I wasn't sure if what I was feeling toward him was anything more than admiration. It wasn't an instant spark—it was a slow, steady burn. But with each conversation and every shared laugh, I found myself drawn to him more and more.

As it turns out, the feeling was mutual. Though he was subtle at first, I could see it in the way he lingered after meetings and in the small, thoughtful ways he made room for me in his day. Danie saw it, too—probably before either of us—and she wasn't shy about nudging us a little closer at every opportunity.

Every fall, the school organized a weekend retreat for all the teachers and staff—a time to step away, breathe in the mountain air, and create memories together. Those weekends were always filled with laughter, good food, and the kind of bonding that felt effortless.

Danie and Mirna managed every detail—from working with vendors to finalizing the venue—ensuring everything unfolded beautifully. Danie, especially, poured her energy into the room assignments. Her careful planning set the stage for a seamless retreat at Le Montcel, a picturesque mountain hideaway in the cool Kenscoff hills, where pine trees framed breathtaking views of Port-au-Prince below.

But Danie had more than logistics in mind. In true matchmaker-on-a-mission fashion, she deliberately placed my cottage right next to Art's. I imagine her smiling as she wrote the list, confident that the magic of the mountains would do the rest. And she was right—those quiet evenings at Le Montcel, with the crisp night air and the stars scattered above us, became the backdrop for something more than a work retreat. They became the beginning of us.

After the retreat, Danie was eager to know everything, of course. *Did we talk a lot? Did he make a move? Did I feel a connection— something more? Any chemistry?*

When I got home, I wanted to call Art, but I didn't want to seem too eager. So, I came up with a reason: I pretended to need another staff member's phone number and called to ask if he had it. What started as a simple request turned into a much longer conversation. We talked well past the exchange of that phone number, and soon, our evening chats became a routine. Talking to him felt effortless—our conversations sometimes diving into the tiniest details of our days, yet never feeling mundane.

Art eventually asked me on our first official "date"—a pool day at Montana, a stunning hotel nestled in the hills of Pétion-Ville. With all the confidence in the world, he reminded me to "bring my bathing suit." I had just gotten my hair braided, and I thought, *Clearly, this man has no idea about Black girl hair and water.*

So, when we arrived, I conveniently "forgot" my bathing suit. While he swam, I sat at the edge, dipping my toes in the water, thinking, *This will be interesting to explain.* Still, we spent the day by the pool, soaking up the Haitian sun. We had a lovely time and were already looking forward to our next date.

Back at school, our students would hum wedding songs every time they saw us together. In their eyes, if two people shared a meal, they were practically married. In my Haitian mind, we were nearly ready to send out invitations. But to Art, an American, we were still in the "getting to know each other" phase.

During one of our first few lunches together at the school cafeteria, Art did some quick math and said, "Let me guess—you're twenty-four years old?" His reaction when I nodded was priceless.

I had to laugh. Twenty-four? He was four years off! But I wasn't about to correct him—better to let him think I looked that young! We exchanged pleasantries, and that was that. But his comment stuck with me, reminding me of the typical path American students follow into adulthood. Most Americans finish college by twenty-two, so it made sense that he thought I was twenty-four, having told him I graduated two years earlier.

What he didn't know was that my journey had followed a different pattern from the start. Nothing in my life had happened "on time." I often felt like I was behind in everything. Yet, in those moments, I reminded myself that God's timing is always perfect.

In the spring of 2009, I invited Art to visit my hometown of St. Michel. As we walked through the village, people stared at us—well, mostly at him. At one point, we overheard two locals trying to figure us out. One guy suggested I was from Jamaica, while the other was convinced Art was Canadian. As they debated in Creole, Art turned around, greeted them in fluent Creole, and introduced me. The shock on their faces was priceless.

One of the men asked Art directly, "So, is she your girlfriend?"

Art replied in typical American fashion, "Well … we're getting to know each other."

In Haitian culture, there's no "getting to know each other." You're either together or you're not! One of the men then asked me a list of qualifications: Did I have a job? Did I have my own home or apartment? Did I have any kids?

Finally, satisfied, he turned to both of us and boldly said to Art, "So, if she's not your girlfriend …" then he looked at me and said, "Can I come live with you?"

Well, that woke Art up. He turned to the guy and said, "Actually, she *is* my girlfriend." We joke to this day that it took a stranger offering to move in with me to get Art to define our relationship.

We had a lovely time in St. Michel. Showing Art my beloved village and the people I love so much was special to me. When we got back to Port-au-Prince, Art invited me to dinner and finally asked me, officially, if I wanted to be his girlfriend. I answered, "About time!"

Dating someone from a different culture came with unique challenges for both of us. As I got to know Art more, I realized he was weighing a lot of factors. "I knew I loved you, Miquette," he said to me once as we talked about our dating story. "However, I wasn't sure how long I wanted to stay in Haiti. Making a year-to-year commitment there was comfortable, but when I looked at marriage, I wondered if I was ready to marry a country as well as a beautiful woman." I'm so glad I was patient with him as we figured out our story.

The truth is, there were many questions we each had to answer honestly: "Am I ready to live in another country?" "How will we handle family traditions?" But as we navigated it all, we found common ground, especially in faith and family values.

THE DAY THE EARTH SHATTERED

Tuesday, January 12, 2010, started like any other day. As a school nurse, and teacher of biology and anatomy, I had planned to administer a biology exam to my sophomore class and later attend my weekly Rotary meeting at the Montana Hotel at 5:30 p.m.

The morning was peaceful. I woke up, read my Bible, prayed, and savored my morning coffee before heading off to work. The day unfolded smoothly. My students were well-behaved, I administered the exam, and later, I joined my workout group for our daily session in the school gym. By mid-afternoon, I was back to grading papers, sitting on the steps of our school chapel. The building was simple, a one-story structure with a small, covered foyer, located near the bustling Delmas main road.

Behind the school's protective wall, merchants lined the streets selling everything from bread and juice to car parts and shoes. The noise of the street was chaotic—a mix of passionate conversations, loud singing, and occasional fights. Oddly enough, I found solace in the chaos as I graded my students' exams. One particular student caught my attention; he had struggled for most of the semester, but this time, he had excelled. I was so proud of him. As I prepared to write his grade—a well-deserved A minus—I was filled with excitement, even planning to call his parents to inform them how well their son had done in this biology exam.

Then it happened …

A loud, deafening rattle erupted, and the world around me began to sway violently from left to right. Confused and disoriented, I stood up, stepping away from the chapel, but the ground beneath me felt like water, shifting uncontrollably. It was then that I realized—I was experiencing an earthquake.

Within seconds, chaos consumed the streets. Screams echoed through the air, blending with the sound of crumbling buildings.

I ran to the center of the school, hoping to check on everyone. Faces of shock mirrored my own as we tried to process what was happening. I opened the school gate and looked toward the main road, and what I saw will haunt me forever.

Across the street, a wall had collapsed on a teacher walking home. People rushed to help, desperately trying to lift the massive concrete slab pinning him to the ground. I joined them, attempting to stop the bleeding, but deep down, I knew it wasn't enough. The internal injuries were likely far worse. That man was the first casualty I witnessed after the earthquake, and his lifeless body marked the beginning of a nightmare.

The scenes that followed are etched into my mind. Hearing people screaming from beneath slabs of heavy concrete, their desperate voices crying out for help, was unlike anything I had ever experienced. Seeing little boys, girls, and even tiny babies pleading for aid while trapped or injured was unbearable.

I found Art on the soccer field just moments after the earthquake hit. The ground had stopped shaking, but everything around us still felt unsteady. Dust hung in the air. Screams echoed in the distance. We stood there, dazed and dejected, our eyes scanning the horizon, trying to make sense of what had just happened. In that moment, we had no idea of the magnitude of what was unfolding—only that life as we knew it had just changed.

We didn't say much. We didn't have to. The fear on both our faces said everything. My heart was racing with worry for my family, and without hesitation, Art offered to come with me as I ran toward my parents' house. Fueled by adrenaline and panic, I sprinted ahead—outrunning even Art, who was an experienced runner.

As we moved through the streets, the devastation became more overwhelming. Multi-story buildings lay flattened like pancakes. Cries of agony rose from every direction. People stumbled through the rubble, calling out names, desperately searching for loved ones. It felt like running through a nightmare—one we couldn't wake up from. But through it all, Art stayed close behind, a steady presence in a world suddenly torn apart.

When I finally reached my family's home and saw them alive, I fell to my knees in gratitude, thanking God for His mercy. My teenage nephew, Cleeford, had sprained his ankle while jumping to safety during the earthquake—an injury we could live with. My niece, Nadège, had escaped her collapsing school with cuts and bruises, but she was alive. God had spared them, and for that, I was profoundly thankful.

As the minutes passed, the magnitude of what had just happened began to sink in. A 7.0 magnitude earthquake had ravaged my beloved land. Though the true death toll would never be known, estimates ranged between 300,000 to 350,000 lives lost. Entire neighborhoods were reduced to rubble in just thirty seconds.

It wasn't until later that I realized how narrowly I had cheated death. Had the earthquake struck just forty-seven minutes later, I would have been in the basement of the Montana Hotel for my Rotary meeting, buried beneath its remains. The Montana was a prestigious, four-star hotel with seven floors and 145 rooms. It was known for hosting celebrities, dignitaries, and events, making it a hub of activity in Port-au-Prince. The hotel, once a symbol of luxury and strength, had been utterly destroyed, taking with it countless lives. Many people assumed I was dead, including friends from Detroit Lakes and my alma mater in Moorhead, as communication was nonexistent afterward.

The days, weeks, and months that followed were a blur of heartache and resilience. Nights were spent under the stars, too afraid to sleep indoors. As a nurse, I did everything I could to help the injured, but the sheer number of lives lost, and the overwhelming needs left me feeling powerless. What haunted me most was witnessing major surgeries performed without anesthesia, the screams of patients slicing through the air, their pain tangible and unforgettable. No matter how much I did, it never felt like enough.

Yet, even in the face of tragedy, I witnessed the unwavering faith and resilience of the Haitian people. Strangers embraced in comfort, communities stood together, and voices rose in praise to God, despite the sorrow. Haiti—wounded but unshaken—showed me the beauty that can emerge from the ashes.

Hearing the people recite from Psalm 46: "Therefore we will not fear, though the earth give way and the mountains fall into the heart of the sea" was profoundly powerful, a testament to their unwavering trust in God's presence.

January 12, 2010, was the day the earth shattered—but it was also the day I saw the hand of God sparing my life. Through the nightmare, I saw the strength of my people and the undeniable presence of God in the midst of devastation.

CHAPTER 23

Family

BEFORE MAKING ANY serious decisions about our future together, Art had several heartfelt conversations with his family about me. He deeply respected his parents and valued their wisdom, so he wanted to hear their honest thoughts.

One particular conversation left a lasting impression.

He went back to the States for a visit and began talking to his dad about me. His dad quietly listened for a while and then said, "Son, let me get this straight. Miquette loves the Lord, has a great relationship with Jesus Christ, runs a non-profit, has her nursing degree, loves kids, likes a lot of the same things as you, is a beautiful woman … so what exactly do *you* add to the relationship?"

A good jolt of humbleness and perspective went a long way!

On July 18, 2011, after about two years of dating, I flew to Ohio to visit Art's family, completely unaware that this day would change my life forever.

The moment I stepped off the plane at Canton Airport, I spotted him waiting for me. We made our way to the car, and as he reached for the trunk to put my luggage inside, my eyes landed on something unexpected—a beautiful ring resting on his Bible. My heart skipped a beat.

Before I could fully process what was happening, Art dropped to one knee right there in the parking lot and asked me to marry him. Without a second thought, I shouted, "YES!"

The world around us seemed to pause for just a moment—then erupted with applause and cheers from passersby who had witnessed the surprise proposal.

Planning our wedding was both exciting and deeply emotional. As a little girl, I had always dreamed of being part of a wedding, but that opportunity never came—until now. And this time, I wasn't just attending. I was the bride, preparing to marry my soulmate.

Following Art's proposal in Ohio, I returned to Minnesota, where I began shopping for my wedding dress. Though John and Mary still lived in Minnesota, and I had been away in Haiti, their support remained unwavering. They had become like a second set of parents to me, and they extended that same love and generosity in countless ways—including offering to pay for my wedding dress. It was a simple gesture, but one that spoke volumes about how deeply they cared and how closely they continued to walk this journey with me.

I visited a few bridal shops and tried on dress after dress. It didn't take long before I found the one—a simple yet elegant off-shoulder white gown. The moment I stepped into it, I felt it: This was the dress I would walk down the aisle in. I said yes to the dress with a full heart and tears in my eyes.

Art and I chose the Palm in Pétion-Ville as our wedding venue because of its beautiful setting and thoughtful amenities. It was a serene residential compound blended with an event space, surrounded by tall palm trees, flowering plants, and lush greenery that made the entire place feel like a private oasis. A sparkling pool sat at the center of the backyard, adding a calm, reflective beauty to the atmosphere. It was the perfect place to say, "I do."

As I planned the ceremony, my heart couldn't help but wander back to what my mama had told me about her wedding day. She and my father had nothing extravagant—just love and the will to begin a life together. They served bread and cola as their main course, a modest celebration grounded in hope and commitment. Thinking about it brought tears to my eyes. It reminded me that a wedding is not measured by its glamour but by the depth of the love it celebrates.

Standing in the middle of the Palm, surrounded by the beauty of the moment, I carried my parents' legacy with me. From bread and cola to a garden oasis, I was living out a dream they had once prayed for. This was the fulfillment of generations of quiet, faithful love.

October 15, 2011, was simply beautiful—filled with anticipation, love, and the promise of a lifetime together. Our wedding started right on time at 3 p.m. and lasted just forty-five minutes, which meant that a few friends, expecting the typical delay, missed the ceremony entirely!

To ensure everyone felt included, my dear friend Karyne Alexis translated the ceremony into Creole for the non-English speakers, bridging the language gap with warmth and grace. Art's father had the honor of reading Scripture, his voice steady and heartfelt, grounding us in the sacredness of the moment.

Jeff Graham, a pastor and colleague from work, officiated the ceremony, adding a personal and heartfelt touch. Surrounded by family and friends, Art and I stood side by side and said, "I do." It was a day overflowing with love, joy, and the presence of those who had shaped our journey.

By my side stood my sister, Farah, as my maid of honor, her constant support shining through. Cherline and Danie (a.k.a. "the matchmaker") completed my wedding party, standing with me as I stepped into this new chapter of life. On Art's side, his cousin Chrissy and best man, Nate, traveled to be part of the joyous occasion, a testament to the deep friendships and bonds that had brought us here.

Beyond the powerful declaration of "I now pronounce you husband and wife," I will never forget the honor of being walked down the aisle by both John Lee and my papa, each holding one of my arms—A moment that still brings tears to my eyes.

Seeing my mama, Rose, and Art's mother, Nancy, lighting the unity candle together was another profoundly touching moment. Though they didn't share a common language, their gesture spoke volumes—love is the ultimate universal language. Having both of our parents there made the day so meaningful and memorable as we began our life together.

The reception that followed was a true feast, with the perfect blend of Haitian and American cuisine, rice and beans, pasta, different types of meats, and a variety of desserts. We'd chosen a location that allowed us to hold both the ceremony and reception seamlessly in one place, and by 9 p.m., everything was wrapped up.

COUNTING MY BLESSINGS

Art and I loved our life as a married couple, settling into our tiny apartment on the school campus. We dreamed of having children but savored our time together, building memories in our cozy home.

A year and a half later, we discovered we were expecting our first child, and we were over the moon. Our joy was matched only by the excitement of my family. My dad, in particular, was ecstatic. He couldn't wait to hold our first child in his arms.

Unlike my mama's children, our first child, Maxwell Arthur, was born on June 28, 2013, in a private hospital in Pétion-Ville. Throughout my pregnancy, we were blessed to have regular doctor visits, which included ultrasounds and proper prenatal care. This experience was a stark contrast to that of my parents, whose children were all born on a dirt floor with no doctor's visits—

including my own birth. I still remember my sister Sandra's reaction when I told her I was having contractions while reading a book.

"Wait, you're having what?" she exclaimed, her eyes bulging like she'd just seen a ghost. "Reading a book while in labor? Are you trying to win the Most Relaxed Birth of the Year Award?"

She wasn't done. When I mentioned that the epidural was working wonders, she grinned and said, "Oh, so this is how rich folks do it, huh? Private room, anesthesiologist on call, and you're over there reading novels like it's story time?"

She laughed and said during her labor, she couldn't even afford Tylenol for the pain. We laughed until tears rolled down our faces. She was genuinely happy for me, her words carrying not just humor, but gratitude for the blessings God had given us.

When Papa held Max for the first time, something in him softened. The deep lines of hardship faded, and for a fleeting moment, his face held only wonder. His calloused hands—worn from years of toil, from carrying burdens I could never fathom—cradled my newborn son with a tenderness that took my breath away.

As he gazed at Max, his eyes were searching, almost reverent, as if discovering a piece of himself in that tiny face. He wasn't just holding his grandson; he was holding a dream, a legacy, a future beyond his own. For that one sacred instant, time stood still. His struggles, his sacrifices, his pain—everything melted away. All that remained was love.

I thank God that Papa not only walked me down the aisle but also met Max before he left this world—just three months later. That moment, his weathered hands tracing Max's delicate features with infinite care is a picture I will never forget.

In 2016, our hearts grew fuller than we ever imagined with the birth of our precious son, Rex Clé. His arrival brought boundless energy, joy, and laughter that continues to light up our lives.

It was a beautiful Monday. I had just finished lunch with my friends and co-workers Pascale, Danie, Rouslyx, Sandra, Phedora, and a few others at work. Feeling a bit tired, I went home around 1 p.m. to rest. However, at 1:30 p.m., my water broke, and I went into labor. I immediately called Art, who was at work, to let him know. He came right away and drove me to the hospital.

Labor was progressing quickly, and the rough, uneven roads— riddled with potholes—only intensified my pain. Although the Maternité de Pétion-Ville was nearby, the drive took thirty ago- nizing minutes that felt like an eternity.

On the way, we called the anesthesiologist to inform her I would need an epidural as soon as I arrived. She got there twenty min- utes later, but those twenty minutes were some of the most pain- ful I had ever endured. I arrived at the hospital by 2:15 p.m., gripping Art's hands so tightly that he still remembers how close I came to breaking them.

Rex was kind to me—his birth was remarkably swift. We were blessed with exceptional prenatal care from the same OB-GYN, Dr. Guichard, who had also delivered Max. Throughout the preg- nancy, I also worked with a doula. Having two experts with such calm and reassuring demeanors made me feel safe, supported, and deeply cared for during the entire experience.

Thankfully, Rex made his entrance into the world so quickly— less than an hour after I arrived at the hospital! By 3:30 p.m., he was in my arms, weighing 6 lbs. 5 oz. It all happened in a blur—a whirlwind of pain, anticipation, and motion—but the joy in that room was beyond words. I sent a picture of Rex to my friends, whom I had just had lunch with two hours earlier, and they couldn't believe it. "Wait ... weren't we just having lunch?"

We laughed so hard. I'm incredibly grateful for how beautifully everything turned out.

It was such a sweet moment to see Max come to meet his little brother—the one who had just made him a big brother. After school, Art brought him to the hospital, stopping by the store on the way so Max could pick out a gift for his new sibling. The way he looked at his little brother was unforgettable—pure love, curiosity, and wonder. It melted my heart.

To honor my papa, we gave Rex the middle name Clé, a tribute to the man who had shaped my life in countless ways.

Just one year later, in the spring of 2017, God's plan for our family unfolded in the most tender and unexpected way. At just four months old, our sweet Raquel Vanessa came into our lives—a radiant blessing wrapped in profound sorrow, heartbreak, redemption, and grace.

Years ago, my mama was asked by a distant relative, Marie Yolette, to raise her eldest daughter, Vanessa. Vanessa was five at the time, and my mama loved her as one of her own. I was already grown at the time, but I was thrilled to gain another little baby sister. Vanessa thrived under my parents' care. She attended an all-English school and became fluent in English. Eventually, she became an English teacher and was passionate about shaping young minds. She was always looking for ways to pay it forward and generously supported those in need around her.

Vanessa first learned that her mother was pregnant when Marie Yolette traveled from Cap-Haïtian to Port-au-Prince to attend Vanessa's wedding in February 2016. The news caught her off guard, but in true Vanessa fashion—selfless, compassionate, and strong—she embraced it with grace. She told her mother she would gladly take the baby once she was born and raise her in the capital. As an English teacher, Vanessa dreamed of teaching her little sister the language early on and giving her a future filled with opportunity and love. She understood how little her mother had to offer while raising a large family, and she was determined to step in—to help, to nurture, to protect.

But Vanessa never got the chance. Just three months after Raquel's birth, she passed away suddenly—without ever meeting the sister she had longed to care for.

Only a month later, Marie Yolette also passed away.

With both mother and sister gone, Raquel—barely four months old—was left in the care of her father, who was already raising several children. Heartbroken and overwhelmed, he made the painful decision to place Raquel for adoption. It was a choice made not from a lack of love but from grief and an inability to provide.

Our hearts broke with the news. But even in the midst of deep sorrow, we sensed God's unmistakable hand. When we were given the opportunity to adopt Raquel, we knew without question: She was meant to be ours.

From the very first moment we held her, she felt like home.

She was the easiest of our three babies—sleeping soundly through the night, unlike her older brothers who needed endless rocking and careful tiptoeing. But she had one sweet requirement: her crocheted "dodo blanket," a gift from her cousin Georgia. That blanket became her constant companion. Without it, no amount of cuddling could calm her.

Even as a baby, music lived in Raquel's soul. She would tap her tiny fingers on my back to the rhythm and sway whenever music played. Her love for dancing began before she could walk, and it continues to bring joy to our home each day.

Her big brothers, Max and Rex, adore her—though Raquel makes sure they know she's a force of her own. She is strong, spirited, joyful, and full of life.

A year after Raquel joined our family, we were met with another wave of grief: Her biological father Richard passed away unexpectedly. Though he wasn't present in her everyday life, his loss was deeply felt. He had loved Raquel in the only way he could— by making the heartbreaking choice to let her go in hopes she would have a better life with us.

Raquel doesn't just carry the love and legacy of Vanessa, Marie Yolette, and Richard in spirit—she carries Vanessa's name as her own. In her eyes, their love shines. In her laughter, their hopes live on.

Raquel is our living proof that even in life's darkest valleys, love still finds a way. And when it does, it changes everything.

Each of our children is a living testament to God's faithfulness and love. They are more than our greatest gifts—they are daily reminders of the incredible journey that brought us here. Not a day goes by that I don't feel overwhelmed with gratitude for the privilege of being their mother. Their love, their smiles, and even their wildest moments are treasures I hold in my heart.

CHAPTER 24

Pay It Forward

TO WHOM MUCH is given, much is required.[4]

When I arrived in the United States in 2000, my life changed in ways I could never have imagined. For the first time, I didn't have to worry about survival—where my next meal would come from or how to pay for school. That freedom gave me something priceless: the ability to dream beyond myself and for others.

As I reflected on the immense blessings in my life, I felt a profound responsibility to give back. People like John and Mary Lee had sacrificed so much to help me break the chains of poverty. Rotary reminded me what it truly meant to live out "Service Above Self." Their generosity became my inspiration—to pay it forward and create opportunities for others to experience hope, dignity, and transformation.

While in the US, the goal had always been to go back to Haiti and help in my own country. Many of my friends, especially those from the Haitian community, thought I was joking. Some even challenged me, saying that once I saw how much I could earn as an RN, my desire to return to Haiti would fade. But I knew that wasn't true. I knew I was called to go back. That certainty never wavered.

During my senior year of college, I began to seriously consider how I could make a difference in Haiti. Growing up there, my focus was solely on survival—fighting daily just to meet my basic needs left little room to think about the broader struggles of my

---

[4] Luke 12:48

people. However, being in the United States created space in my mind and heart to reflect on my country, my people, and the legacy I wanted to leave for Haiti's children.

With this in mind, I did something that may sound bizarre—I googled Haiti. I know it might seem strange to search for a place I had lived my entire life, but what I read shocked me. The statistics on poverty, the misery, and the stark disparity between the haves and the have-nots were overwhelming. It was as if I were seeing my country from a completely new perspective. I had lived in that reality, yet reading about it—analyzing the facts and merging them with my own lived experience—made it hit differently. It came with a realization: I had to do something.

At the time, I was on my way to becoming a nurse, so my first thought was public health. I believed it would be the best way to make a lasting impact. But as I researched, one heartbreaking statistic stood out—countless children all across Haiti couldn't afford an education. We weren't the only ones who struggled with this.

While students in developed countries may see education as an obligation, for many children in Haiti, it's a dream few can afford. Wearing a school uniform and carrying books isn't a rote routine—it's a symbol of hope and opportunity.

Haiti's education system, overseen by the Ministère de l'Éducation Nationale et de la Formation Professionnelle (MENFP) is chronically underfunded. According to World Bank data from 2022, only 1.27 percent of its Gross Domestic Product (GDP) is dedicated to education.[5] Families must cover fees, uniforms, and supplies, forcing impossible choices: feed their children or send them to school. Often, they can't afford to do either.

[5] "Haiti Education Spending, Percent of GDP - Data, Chart." TheGlobalEconomy.com. Accessed August 21, 2025. https://www.theglobaleconomy.com/Haiti/Education_spending/.

The impact is undeniable. According to World Bank, "more than 250,000 children aged 6–11 and about 65,000 youth aged 12–14 are not enrolled in school for financial or other reasons."[6] These numbers tell a heartbreaking story—one of potential lost far too soon.

I remembered my own story—being in the fifth grade when my dreams of becoming a nurse were nearly crushed because my parents couldn't afford 100 gourdes, less than $1, for my tuition. That memory planted a seed in my heart: *What if other children are losing their dreams for the same reason?*

That question shifted my prayers.

The more I prayed, the clearer it became—education was the key. Nelson Mandela's words struck me like a lightning bolt, awakening me to the urgency of this truth: "Education is the most powerful weapon which you can use to change the world." His message wasn't just inspiring; it was a call to action. Education had to be the priority.

I knew in my heart that this was the path I was meant to take. Wanting guidance, I spoke with John and Mary about my vision, eager to hear their thoughts. As always, they supported me wholeheartedly. They understood why I felt so strongly about providing education to children like me—children whose futures depended on opportunities they might never receive without help. They had seen firsthand how the gift of education had transformed my life, and they believed in my calling just as much as I did.

---

[6] World Bank Group. "'One Day I Will Be...' - School Attendance and a Keen Interest in Learning Are Priorities for Many Young Haitians." World Bank, November 15, 2023. https://www.worldbank.org/en/news/feature/2023/11/15/school-attendance-and-a-keen-interest-in-learning-are-priorities-for-many-young-haitians?utm_source=chatgpt.com.

In 2007, that conviction became Teach Haiti, a 501©3 nonprofit dedicated to ensuring that no child loses their potential because of something as small as 100 gourdes. It empowers the next generation of Haitian leaders, giving them tools to see the beauty in themselves, their country, and their God-given potential. Our mission is "To provide a comprehensive biblical education that empowers children to emerge from poverty, impact their community, and lead with integrity."

THE BEGINNING OF TEACH HAITI

In 2007, I began fundraising with what I thought was a bold goal: to send ten children to school in Haiti. I honestly wasn't sure if I could raise enough, but I was determined to try. To my surprise, by June of that same year—just a few weeks before leaving for Haiti—I had raised enough funds to provide scholarships for 41 children.

The impact was even greater than I imagined. We partnered with several reputable schools in Port-au-Prince and St. Michel, and I quickly learned to negotiate on behalf of our students. I would say to the school directors: "If I enroll five students in your school, would you give me the sixth one for free?" To my amazement, many agreed. This strategy allowed us to stretch donor dollars even further and enroll more students than we had ever dreamed possible.

The process of joining the program was simple but meaningful. Any child could apply. Once an application was received, it was reviewed by a committee in Haiti made up of parents, pastors, and community leaders. The applicant and their parents were then interviewed. Once accepted, families were informed of the program standards: students would be provided with everything they needed for school—books, supplies, tuition—but they were expected to maintain at least a "B" average and be a role model in their school and community.

It was always difficult, because hundreds of students qualified, yet we could only help a fraction of them. Still, from 2007 to 2010, Teach Haiti faithfully provided scholarships to dozens of children every year.

THE TURNING POINT

Then came the earthquake of 2010, a tragedy that shook Haiti and forever changed many lives, including mine. In the midst of the devastation, I felt a strong call: it was time for Teach Haiti to start its own school. I had always dreamed of a place where children could be taught with excellence and care, preparing them not only to succeed in their studies but also to thrive as leaders in their communities.

I shared this vision with our Board of Directors, and as they had always done, they trusted me and gave me the green light. I was overjoyed at the chance to shape the way our students would learn. Unlike my own education in Haiti—where many of my teachers had barely finished high school—I wanted these children to be taught by qualified teachers with college or teaching degrees. I also wanted them to experience what I never had:

- A nutritious meal every single day.

- Physical education and fine arts woven into their curriculum.

- English language instruction starting in preschool, not middle school, because I knew firsthand how knowing English could open doors for children in Haiti.

THE FIRST SCHOOL

Finding a building was a humble but hope-filled experience. I told myself: My sister Sandra happened to have a four-room house in Puits-Blain Port Au prince that had never been rented since before the earthquake. When I asked if we could use it for our first school, she gladly agreed.

We quickly renovated the small house. I had help from our board members in Minnesota, including Tom Klyve, who traveled to Haiti that summer to help get the building ready to receive our first group of students in October 2010. He even brought along much-needed school supplies including classroom decorations, making the classrooms feel bright, welcoming, and full of hope.

Teachers were recruited by word of mouth, and from our pool of scholarship students, we selected 61 who lived nearby to begin this new chapter. We opened our doors with grades 1 through 4, and each year added a new grade until our students reached high school.

TEACH HAITI TODAY

As of now, Teach Haiti operates two campuses—one in my hometown of St. Michel and one in Port-au-Prince—serving more than 650 students. Today, Teach Haiti is recognized as one of the best schools in the country. Our students consistently score among the highest on national state exams in both 9th and 12th grade. Every senior graduating from Teach Haiti receives a full scholarship to attend one year of trade school, because we understand the importance of equipping them with the resources and skills needed to be successful beyond high school.

Through Teach Haiti, we are making sure that their voices will not be silenced by poverty.

That was the beginning of the Teach Haiti School—born out of both tragedy and hope, fueled by faith, trust, and the belief that education could break the chains of poverty for generations to come.

Sharing my story has shifted from being personal to purposeful. Speaking to churches, schools, and organizations like Rotary allowed me to connect others not only to my journey but also to the stories of Haitian children who needed a lifeline. It became clear that advocating for education wasn't just important—it was my calling.

Since its founding, Teach Haiti has grown far beyond what I ever imagined. We provide scholarships, school supplies, uniforms, and mentorship, empowering children to stay in school and thrive. We nurture their talents, build their confidence, and inspire them to lead lives of purpose and integrity.

In 2013, we began construction on our second campus. Building a school in my hometown of St. Michel has been one of my greatest joys. The school welcomed its first group of preschoolers in September 2016. Many of the parents who send their children there are people I grew up with—neighbors, friends, and families who knew my struggles firsthand. For them, my return represents a symbol of hope.

They tell me, "If Miquette, Rose and Bos Clé's daughter, can come back and create change, then our children can have a better future, too." For them, my journey is proof of what God's grace and determination can achieve.

Access to education is a fundamental right for every child, regardless of their socioeconomic status. Education is about so much more than learning letters and numbers—It's about dignity. It's about restoring their voices. It's about affirming that every child is worthy of being invested in, that they deserve a seat at the table.

That belief has stayed with me. It's why I fight so hard to ensure that every student, no matter their circumstances, has access to education. Because I know what it feels like to be on the outside looking in. I know the ache of watching others walk toward opportunity while feeling left behind. And I also know the profound, life-changing joy of finally being let inside—of being seen, valued, and given a chance. No child should have to wait for that chance.

There's a story I often share—one that still haunts me. A girl named Dina arrived at school one day, visibly ill. Concerned, her teacher gently asked why she hadn't stayed home to rest. Dina's response silenced her teacher. With her eyes lowered and shame etched across her face, she whispered, "Miss, if I don't come to school, where will I get my food for the day?"

For Dina, school wasn't just a place to learn—it was survival. Her story is a stark reminder of why Teach Haiti exists: yes, to provide education but to also offer hope, opportunity, and dignity to children who deserve more than just a chance—they deserve a future.

Teach Haiti has impacted over one thousand students so far. We have countless stories of transformation—stories like that of a young woman named Valentine. She was on the verge of abandoning her dream of finishing high school due to financial hardship. But Teach Haiti stepped in, providing the support she needed to complete her education.

Today, she is a bona fide professional—a teacher, an author, and a friend—who has not only built a successful career but has also helped countless members of her family gain financial freedom.

Most importantly, she is now one of my closest friends. She has dedicated countless hours to Teach Haiti, serving as the best ambassador we could ever ask for. Her passion, commitment, and generosity have made a lasting impact—not only on the organization but on the lives of so many students who now have the same opportunities she once received.

And she is just one of many. There are so many stories like hers—stories of resilience, opportunity, and lives forever changed.

Poverty blinds us to beauty, consumes our focus, devours dreams, and tries to silence our voices. Education restores what poverty steals. It equips children to see beyond their circumstances, to imagine brighter futures, and to build better lives.

Teach Haiti stands as a testament to what's possible when generous people, like the Lees, take a leap of faith to help a child in need. It's a reminder that no matter where we begin, destitute isn't destiny. There is always hope—a hope that inspires big dreams, even when they seem insurmountable.

Growing up, dreaming of becoming a nurse felt like climbing an impossible mountain, yet that hope carried me forward. When nurtured, hope has the power to transform not just one life but entire communities, igniting a ripple effect of change and possibility.

FROM HUMBLE BEGINNINGS

In January 2017, I received a letter that left me speechless. I had been named the recipient of Concordia College's Sent Forth Mission Award, an honor reserved for alumni who make a meaningful impact in the world and embody the college's mission to "influence the affairs of the world." I felt deeply honored and overwhelmed. This was a validation of my life's work and a testament to every step I had taken to make a difference in Haiti through education.

Not long after, another letter arrived—this time from Dr. William Craft, the college president. As I read it, my heart pounded. He was inviting me to be the 2017 commencement speaker. I couldn't believe it. I handed the letter to my husband, Art, asking if I had read it correctly. He looked up, eyes wide, and said, "Wow, honey, they want *you* to be their commencement speaker."

What? Me? A commencement speaker at Concordia? The thought was staggering. I eagerly replied to Dr. Craft, accepting with joy and humility. I've shared my story countless of times, always speaking from the heart without notes. But this moment felt too big, too important. I was standing on one of the biggest stages of my life, about to address thousands of people.

As I took the stage, memories of my past washed over me. I thought of that poor girl from St. Michel, shamed and humiliated because of our poverty. I never could have imagined that one day, I would stand here, honored, celebrated, and delivering the most important speech of the event.

During my speech, I spoke from the depths of my experience, emphasizing that one's background should never limit one's potential. I urged the class of 2017 to seize opportunities now, to make a difference in their hometowns, communities, and beyond. I encouraged them to use their education to uplift others, to bless and influence the world in ways big and small.

As I finished speaking, something magical happened. The crowd rose to their feet, clapping and cheering. I stood there, overwhelmed, tears streaming down my face, realizing how far I'd come—from a child struggling to survive in St. Michel to a woman inspiring the next generation of graduates.

In 2020, my high school, Oak Grove Lutheran School, honored me with the Living the Mission Award, a distinction that holds deep meaning. This award recognizes alumni, parents, employees, and friends whose lives exemplify the school's mission: "To express God's love by nurturing students for academic achievement, lifelong Christian commitment, and loving service throughout the world."

Receiving this award felt like coming full circle, as it celebrated not only my achievements but also the values instilled in me during my senior year there. The recipients of this honor are chosen for their selfless contributions; their generosity of time, talents, and resources; and for living out their faith with humility and grace.

To be recognized among this group of extraordinary individuals was both humbling and affirming. It served as a reminder that the seeds planted during my time at Oak Grove had taken root and grown into something greater—a life devoted to service, to nurturing others, and to sharing God's love with the children of Haiti.

In January 2025, I received another award that was incredibly meaningful to me. I was truly in awe when the Network of Haitian Women Models and Inspirers (REFEHMI) selected me as one of their 50 Inspiring Women in the Country. Their mission is to shine a spotlight on women who are working toward a better Haiti—one where all children have the opportunity to live with dignity.

This award was especially profound, as it represented recognition from my own country for my efforts. It was both an honor and a powerful motivation to continue the work I am so passionate about.

Every day, I count my blessings, each one a testament to the journey from the crushing depths of poverty to a life filled with hope and purpose. I remember the sting of being sent home from school because my parents couldn't afford the fees, the shame of feeling like my family's struggles were on display for everyone to see, and the helplessness that no child should ever carry.

But I also remember the spark of hope that refused to die, even in the darkest moments. That hope, fragile yet unyielding, carried me forward.

Today, as I watch my children Max, Rex, and Raquel grow up in a life so different from my own—with full plates, safe homes, and endless opportunities—I am overwhelmed with gratitude. They don't know the hunger or uncertainty I knew, and for that, I am endlessly thankful.

And today, when I see my mama, I see a woman filled with hope and renewal. The years that poverty stole from her have been softened. She often tells me how she remembers those hard days but now cries with gratitude instead of pain. She is still the strongest woman I know.

These blessings fuel my resolve to ensure that no child, no mother, no family has to endure what we did. That's why I tell my story, and that's why I started Teach Haiti—to provide education, inspire hope, and help break the cycle of poverty for generations to come. It's my way of honoring the hardships, tears, and triumphs of my journey and paying forward the grace and generosity that changed my life.

Believing in the power of God is what sustained me through the hardest times. I've learned that we are His masterpiece, created with purpose, and that He wants the best for us. When I doubted my worth or my future, my faith reminded me that I was not alone—and neither are you.

To anyone reading this who may feel stuck in despair, I want you to know: Don't stop dreaming. I was just a poor girl with impossible dreams, but those dreams carried me forward, one step at a time, to where I am today. You, too, can make it happen.

Your story isn't over. Your dreams, no matter how distant they feel, can lead you to a future brighter than you can imagine. Trust in God's plan, hold tight to hope, and never stop believing in the beauty of what lies ahead. You are capable, you are loved, and you are destined for more than you can dream.

Together, we can create a world where no one is defined by their beginnings, however humble, but by the hope, determination, and dreams that carry them forward.

PHOTOS

Miquette in front of her one room house in Port au Prince. Front row left, niece Nadege, nephew Johnbenson, cousin Vanessa. Back row, left, Mama Rose, middle Miquette, and sister Beatrice

Rose, Miquette and John, 1999

Miquette with her papa, 2008

Miquette's Mom Mama Rose

Miquette with Farah left and Cherline right

Miquette High School Graduation from Oak Grove, 2002

John and Mary at Miquette College Graduation 2006

Miquette with Mommy
Carme at her College
Graduation, 2006

Right Miquette with her
College friend Osaki

Wedding, Miquette and Art

Wedding, Art and Miquette

From right, John, Mama Rose, Mary and Miquette

Miquette with John and
Mary Lee

Miquette's mom Rose with
John and Mary Lee

Miquette with Teach Haiti students in St. Michel

Teach Haiti School in St. Michel

Front row from left Sandra, Miquette, Rose. Back row left Pidens and Isaac

Miquette's mom and her grandchildren

Miquette with mom Rose, sisters Beatrice, Sandra and brother Isaac

Left_ Sandra, Miquette, Rose, Camisha, Beatrice

Miquette's mom Rose, left is sister Farah

Left_ Miquette, Cherline and with her husband Mathew
and Rose

Miquette's mom with grandchild Cherline

Miquette with her Mama, Rose

Miquette buying mangos on her way from St. Michel

Miquette with her mom in Washington DC

Miquette's family, Art, Max, Rex, Raquel

Miquette's three children.
Right Max, Raquel and Rex

Right back row Miquette,
Art's dad, Art sr. Art's
mom, Nancy and Art,
Front row: right Rex,
middle Max and Raquel

Miquette, delivering Key note at Rotary Zone 30 & 31,
Hunstville, AL

Miquette delivering a
keynote speak at a Rotary
District Conference

Miquette deliving the
commencement speech
at Concordia College, May
2017

ACKNOWLEDGEMENTS

I WOULD LIKE to thank the many people who have shaped me and contributed to the realization of this book.

First and foremost, I thank my God and Savior, Jehovah Jireh, for His unending grace and provision.

To my husband, Art—thank you for your constant encouragement and amazing support throughout this journey.

To my children, Max, Rex, and Raquel—you inspire me every day. Thank you for giving me the space and understanding I needed to complete this work.

To my mother—thank you for embodying the truth that *destitute isn't destiny*. Your strength and resilience have shaped the very core of who I am.

To my papa—though gone, you loved your children with every fiber of your being. Your memory continues to guide and strengthen me.

To John and Mary—thank you for treating me like your own daughter and for changing the very trajectory of my life. Your love, generosity, and belief in me have made all the difference.

To my brothers and sisters, Beatrice, Sandra, Pidens, Isaac, Farah and Camisha—I am forever grateful for your love and support.

To my nieces and nephews, Cherline, Johnbenson, Nadège, Faridie, Santia, Cleeford, Hondjy, Djaina, Guervens, Adams, Nicka, Christian, Christopher and Mateo—your presence fills my life with joy.

To my host brothers, Dan and Carl—thank you for welcoming me into your lives.

To my dear friends—Danie Desrosiers, Eddy & Mirna Beneche, Valentine Vilcin, Pascale Girault, Rouslyx Fardin, Anouse Norvilus, Guerlande Charles, Chantale Denie, Mirtha Charles, Joanna Dols, Kathy Coyle, Chris Dias, and Amanda Turcotte—thank you for your encouragement and friendship.

To Dr. William Craft and Anne Craft—thank you for your inspiration, guidance, and belief in me.

To Michelle and Shawn Hearn—thank you for investing in my professional life.

To Gladys Thomas—thank you for being a role model and for giving so many children in Haiti a fighting chance for their voices to be heard.

To Gail Kotschevar, Polly Kloster, Jean Bokinskie, Marc Langseth, Vicki Welke, and Jack Rydell—thank you for investing in my educational journey.

To Sharon Josephson, the Noon Rotary Club of Detroit Lakes, and the Pétion-Ville Rotary Club—thank you for taking a chance on me.

To our Teach Haiti teachers, staff, and Mr. Billy—thank you for your dedication in making sure our students are equipped for success.

To the Teach Haiti Board of Directors—thank you for believing in making the voices of Haitian children louder than poverty.

And to the many others who have walked alongside me—thank you. Your encouragement has been a steady source of strength, and I carry each of you with me in these words.

Thank you for walking this journey with me. My story is just one thread in a much larger tapestry of hope, resilience, and transformation. The work continues, and together, we can *generate the change*.

If you're ready to learn more about Teach Haiti and the incredible impact education is making in the lives of children, I invite you to visit www.teachhaiti.org.

To book Miquette for a speaking engagement or event, visit www.miquettemcmahon.com or email mcmahonmiquette@gmail.com.

Mèsi!